EXPLORING THE SADDLEBAG *of* CLASSIC METHODISM

Vic Reasoner

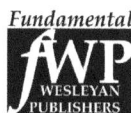

Fundamental

fWP
WESLEYAN
PUBLISHERS

2120 Culverson Ave
Evansville, IN 47714-4811

TABLE of CONTENTS

EXPLORING THE SADDLEBAG *of* CLASSIC METHODISM

It is my hope that we can rediscover the rich, biblical-based theology of early Methodism and appropriate its dynamic for our growth. The next Methodism must build on the foundation laid by the founders rather than the liberal foundation of the previous Methodism which collapsed.

Thus, in order to move forward we must go back to the sources. *Ad fontes* is a Latin phrase meaning back "to the primary sources." What follows is an introduction to classic Methodist teaching and then an exploration of classic Methodist literature.

Revisionist Methodism holds to an evolutionary view of doctrine. For them, newer is truer because it reflects the current theologically correct trends. Thomas Oden described as "modern chauvinists"

> those who have decided that there is precious little worth learning from any premodern voice. They assume the intrinsic inferiority of all premodern texts and the intrinsic superiority of

all modern methods of investigation of those texts.[1]

Evangelicals outside the Methodist tradition tend to disregard classic Methodist literature because they assume it is liberal, like many contemporary Methodist theologians.

Before a survey of classic Methodist literature, I want to summarize their emphasis. The Methodist revival of the eighteenth century was essentially a rediscovery of apostolic Christianity. While there have been other restorationist movements, they all tend to be reductionary — speaking in tongues, a particular mode of baptism, or a prescribed form of church government — will restore apostolic Christianity. Methodism affirmed the three ecumenical confessions of Christian faith — the Apostles' Creed, the Nicene Creed, and the Athanasian Creed.

Classic Methodism preached the full gospel. Wesley argued for liberty concerning nonessentials,[2] but he also believed there were fundamental Christian doctrines which must be maintained.

As twenty-first century classic Methodists . . .

We affirm the full inspiration, inerrancy, and authority of Scripture.

The purpose of inspiration was to insure infallibility. Wesley preached, "'All Scripture is given by inspiration

---

[1]Oden, *Life in the Spirit*, 469.

[2]Wesley, "Catholic Spirit," Sermon #39.

of God' (consequently all Scripture is infallibly true)."[3] It is impossible for God to lie (Titus 1:2). If God communicated truth through the inspiration of the Holy Spirit and if the prophets and apostles got it down right, then Scripture is authoritative because it is the Word of God.

The doctrine of biblical inerrancy means that the human authors accurately recorded what God conveyed to them. If they got it wrong, then the Holy Spirit failed in the process of inspiration. Wesley understood what was at stake when he wrote, "Nay, if there be any mistakes in the Bible there may as well be a thousand. If there be one falsehood in that book, it did not come from the God of truth."[4] He wrote that his foundation was the Bible. He said he followed it in all things, both great and small.[5] He cautioned, "Believe nothing they say unless it is clearly confirmed by plain passages of Holy Writ."[6]

We affirm the being, triune essence, and attributes of God, as well as his role as creator and governor.

Thus, we reject theistic evolution or *evolutionary creati-onism* as essentially updated deism which classic Methodism opposed. We also affirm divine sovereignty which is opposed by process theology.

---

[3]Wesley, "The Means of Grace," Sermon #16, 3.8.

[4]Wesley, *Journal*, 24 July 1776.

[5]Wesley, *Journal*, 5 June 1766.

[6]Wesley, "Sermon on the Mount, XII," 3.9.

We affirm the dual nature and atoning work of Christ.

We affirm the dual nature of Christ as fully God and fully man, who offered himself as a substitutionary atonement for the whole race. The basis of our salvation is the grace of God through the atonement of Jesus Christ. The atonement is the heart of the gospel. Paul declared, "May I never boast except in the cross of our Lord Jesus Christ" (Gal 6:14). "Christ died for us" (Rom 5:8) is the most basic statement of the atonement.

The atonement is the satisfaction of God's justice. When we believe on the Lord Jesus, who has borne the penalty for our sins, God accepts Christ as our substitute and us as his children. We are redeemed from the bondage of sin and are reconciled with God. The atonement of Christ reveals the love of God, the wisdom of God, and turns away the wrath of God. According to Eldon Dunlap,

> the entire theological enterprise of early Methodism was motivated by an evangelical zeal. The salvation of souls was their passion, and salvation rooted firmly in the reality and efficacy of the Atonement. The Atonement was the heart of their theology; it was the theme of their preaching; and it was the practical ground of their Christian living and hope of glory.[7]

Wesley wrote, "Nothing in the Christian system is of greater consequence than the doctrine of Atonement. It is

---

[7]Dunlap, "Methodist Theology in Great Britain," 100.

properly the distinguishing point between Deism and Christianity."[8]

The atonement is both extensive and intensive. It is extensive since it is available to all people. It is intensive because it delivers from all sin. The grace of God extends as deeply as we are tainted by sin. Grace includes the forgiveness of sins, but it also means divine empowerment or enablement to keep the commands of Christ.

We affirm the Holy Spirit as the executive of the Godhead.

We affirm the deity and personhood of the Holy Spirit, who inspired the holy Scriptures and administrates the finished redemption of Christ to sinful men and women who are awakened through his agency, justified by faith, and sanctified to the uttermost.

We affirm the historic fall and resulting sinfulness of mankind.

We affirm the unity of mankind, created in the image of God, fallen into sin and depravity in Adam, and restored through the redemption of the Son of God.

Our total inability to save ourselves, is taught throughout the Bible. Apart from enabling grace, the plight of mankind is hopeless. When his disciples asked Jesus who can be saved, he replied, "With man this is impossible, but with God all things are possible" (Matt 19:25-26). This depravity is *total* since it affects the entire

---

[8]Wesley, *Letter* to Mary Bishop, 7 Feb 1778.

being of man: the intellect is darkened, the affections are alienated, and the will is perverted.

We affirm preliminary grace which enables sinners to obey the commands of the gospel.

The grace which appears to everyone is prevenient or preliminary grace. Preliminary grace restores the capacity of every person to accept salvation. This grace creates a temporary condition in which we are enabled to respond to the drawing of the Father.

Preventing, preparatory, or preliminary grace is the grace of God which precedes or comes before human action. Through preliminary grace our faculties are restored in the wake of total depravity, making us savable. God restores conscience, a knowledge of the moral law, an awareness of himself, and the ability to repent and believe. We are awakened, convinced, and convicted.

Calvinism denies such prevenient grace. They divide grace into "effectual grace" for the elect from "common grace" for everyone. Allan Coppedge explained what is at stake:

> The difference between Wesley's prevenient grace and the Calvinists' common grace was that while both provided a restraining influence on the evil in human beings so that society could exist, prevenient grace also restored the capacity of every man to accept salvation, whereas common grace did not.[9]

---

[9]Coppedge, *John Wesley in Theological Debate*, 136.

According to John Fletcher, the ordinary methods of awakening are affliction, Christian conversation and witnessing, and the preaching of the Word.[10] This dawning of preliminary grace is stifled as soon as possible by most people; but God visits every soul, though most forget or deny the experience.[11] Awakening is analogous to conception. Conception will lead to the new birth unless the gestation process is aborted.

Wesley explained that preliminary grace was a doctrine "of no small importance."[12] He exhorted the one who feared God and kept his commandments to keep seeking God until he passed from the faith of a servant to the faith of a son, was born of God, and had the witness of the Spirit.

We affirm free grace.

Wesley ascribed all good to the free grace of God. He denied all natural free will and all human ability prior to God's preliminary grace.[13] Therefore, justification must be by grace through faith alone. The transformation of grace in our lives excludes any personal merit.

However, Methodism rejected the Calvinistic doctrine which represents Christ as becoming a substitute only for the elect, whom God unconditionally predestined

---

[10]Fletcher, *Works*, 4:127.

[11]Wesley, "Scripture Way of Salvation," Sermon #43, 1.1-2.

[12]Wesley, "On the Discoveries of Faith," Sermon #117, ¶ 13-14.

[13]Wesley, *BE Works*, 10:153.

for salvation. It also rejects universalism, holding that preliminary grace is not the new birth. Their emphasis was on free grace, not free will.[14] This grace is free in all and for all.[15]

The issue which divides Wesleyan-Arminians from Calvinism is not grace. The question is whether this grace is irresistible and whether God's election is unconditional. We understand that this preliminary grace appears to everyone unconditionally, but it may be resisted. Those who accept and submit to this initial grace, enabling them to believe on the Lord Jesus Christ, are the elect.

In this theology of grace, Methodism differed from Calvinism on four important points:

• *Salvation is possible for everyone*

We affirm the atonement of Christ is universal in its potential. The decree of salvation applies to all who believe on Christ and who persevere in faith and obedience. The gospel call is both general in its appeal and efficacious for all who believe.

• *God grants everyone the power of contrary choice*

John Fletcher phrased his question to cut through the confusion between libertarian and compatibilistic free will: "Is the will at liberty to choose otherwise than it

---

[14]Cox, *Perfection*, 41; Maddox, *Responsible Grace*, 92.

[15]Wesley, "Free Grace," Sermon #110, ¶ 2.

does, or is it not?"[16] Ultimately, Calvinistic "freedom" amounts to determinism.

God does not relinquish his sovereignty and he has predestined the *consequences* of our free choices. But he also created mankind with true libertarian freedom. Fletcher explained Wesleyan theology in two axioms, "All our salvation is of God in Christ; all our damnation is of ourselves."[17]

- *Faith is God's gift; believing is our responsibility*

Wesley argued that if salvation is by absolute decree, it is not by works, but neither is it by faith. "For *unconditional* decree excludes faith as well as works."[18] We cannot believe without the gift of faith, but saving faith is a volitional human response which God requires from us.

- *God delivers from sin*

Saving grace results in freedom from the guilt, the bondage, and the power of sin. There is also cleansing from the nature and pollution of sin. Preliminary grace works freely in all mankind — if only for a season. Justifying grace is available to all who respond to preliminary grace. And perfecting grace can deliver the justified from all sin. All this is denied by Calvinism.

---

[16]Fletcher, *Works*, 2:452.

[17]Fletcher, *Works*, 1:17.

[18]Wesley, *BE Works*, 13:554. See also Clarke, *Commentary*, 6:439, 1069.

We affirm the function of the law.

The opposite of law is not grace, but lawlessness. A. Skevington Wood said that it was Wesley's "invariable method to present his hearers with the demands of the moral law, before he spoke of the Savior who had paid the price of their release." Wesley urged the evangelical preacher to "preach the law in the strongest, the closest, the most searching manner possible, only intermixing the gospel here and there." Only after sinners were awakened, did Wesley advise the preacher to "mix more and more of the gospel."[19] In his standard sermons, Wesley devoted three sermons to the purpose of the moral law.

- the law defines sin
- the law convicts of sin
- the law even provokes sin
- the law drives us to Christ who alone can save us.

The one thing the law cannot do is save the sinner. Yet it is indispensable as a diagnostic tool. It is like a mirror which reveals our flaws but cannot remove them.

- the law instructs us as believers. It serves as the standard of obedience for Christians.
- the law is a restraint to evil. It provides the order for all aspects of society.

We affirm justification by faith alone and regeneration through the baptism with the Holy Spirit.

---

[19]Wood, *The Burning Heart*, 242.

Classic Methodism maintained the balance between imputed and imparted righteousness, which leads to the obedience of the moral law. Justification is a legal change, while regeneration is a restorative change. Thomas Oden observed that the Protestant reformers emphasized justification, but "the new birth has sometimes been insufficiently emphasized."[20] Baptist theologian A. H. Strong noted,

> It was John Wesley who did the most to establish the doctrine of regeneration. He asserted that the Holy Spirit acts through the truth, in distinction from the doctrine that the Holy Spirit works solely through the ministers and sacraments of the church.[21]

Five acts of grace occur in conversion.

- We are forgiven of all our past sins. We are justified by grace through faith. We are declared to be righteous.
- We are raised from spiritual death and given a new nature. We receive the Holy Spirit who empowers us to live righteously.
- We are set apart from the old life of sin and initially sanctified.
- We are adopted into the family of God.
- We have assurance of our forgiveness and adoption.

---

[20]Oden, *John Wesley's Teachings*, 2:219-220.

[21]Strong, *Systematic Theology*, 816.

We affirm the direct witness of the Spirit.

Methodism advocated the witness of the Spirit, which was sometimes regarded as the distinct Methodist doctrine.[22] It is a present consciousness of forgiveness and acceptance by God. A present tense faith produces a present tense assurance. Wesley preached

> that the Spirit of God does give a believer such a testimony of his adoption that while it is present to the soul he can no more doubt the reality of his sonship than he can doubt of the shining of the sun while he stands full blaze of its beams.[23]

This was also affirmed by Calvinistic Methodists. In 1739 George Whitefield met Howell Harris and the first question Whitefield asked was, "Do you know that your sins are forgiven?" He did not ask, "Do you believe your sins can be forgiven?" or "Do you believe that your sins are forgiven?" but "Do you *know* that your sins are forgiven?"[24]

We affirm the possibility for those who are truly converted to fall from grace if they do not persevere in faith.

---

[22] For a classic expression, see Stackpole, *Evidence of Salvation*.

[23] Wesley, "Witness of the Spirit, I," Sermon #10, 1.12.

[24] Lloyd-Jones, *The Puritans*, 196.

The whole period of life is a state of probation, in every part of which a sinner may repent and turn to God, and in every part of it a believer may give way to sin and fall from grace; and that this possibility of rising, and liability to falling, are essential to a state of trial or probation.[25]

Our security of salvation is conditioned upon maintained faith. While it is possible to lose salvation, it is never necessary. However, once-saved-always-saved is not necessarily true. It takes the same faith to maintain our relationship with Christ as it does to enter into that relationship.

We must keep covenant with God. Our relationship with him is a dynamic relationship that can constantly be improved and can always be forfeited. Wesley was impressed with the phrase from François Fénelon "my progress is without end."[26] Wesley insisted that we cannot possibly stand still. "Unless they continue to watch and pray and aspire after higher degrees of holiness, I cannot conceive not only how they can go forward but how they can keep what they have already received."[27]

Scripture also warns against apostasy. To conclude that those who depart from the faith actually never were elect violates the very concept of apostasy. One cannot abandon what he never possessed. Joseph Benson

---

[25]Etheridge, *Life of Clarke*, 75.

[26]Tuttle, *Mysticism in the Wesleyan Tradition*, 156.

[27]Wesley, *Letter* to Mrs. Pawson, 16 Nov 1789.

preached that growth in grace is the only security against falling from it.[28]

We affirm the need for accountability.

The word *disciple* originally meant to be a student. Discipleship is learning to utilize the means of grace. This is what it means to be *methodistic*.

A spiritual discipline which people use to express their faith and receive God's grace is called a *means of grace*. We must remember that these spiritual disciplines are means, and not the end in themselves. John Wesley taught

> By "means of grace" I understand outward signs, words, or actions, ordained of God, and appointed for this end — to be the ordinary channels whereby he might convey to men, preventing, justifying, or sanctifying grace.[29]

Wesley distinguished between the instituted means of grace which are works of piety ordained by God and the prudential means of grace which are spontaneous, practical works of mercy.

Prayer and fasting, daily Bible reading and the reading of devotional literature, spiritual conversation, public worship and the sacraments, accountability to a small group, and financial giving are all instituted means of grace. While baptism is a sacrament, since it is not repeated, it is not usually listed.

---

[28]Benson, *Sermons*, 7:230-232. Sermon #251.

[29]Wesley, "The Means of Grace," Sermon #16, 2.1.

Works of mercy include feeding the hungry, clothing the naked, entertaining the stranger, visiting those who are sick or imprisoned, instructing the ignorant, awakening the sinner, quickening the lukewarm, comforting those who are struggling, encouraging those who are tempted, and in any way contributing to the saving of souls from death. While we should be zealous for works of piety, Wesley taught that we should be *much more* zealous for works of mercy (Hos 6:6; Matt 9:13, 12:7).

Thus, classic Methodism is a disciplined lifestyle. William Carvosso served as a class leader for sixty years. His *Memoir* written in 1836 is a Methodist classic describing the dynamic of accountability.

In a conversation with Robert Miller in 1783, Wesley was asked what must be done to keep Methodism alive when he was dead. He immediately answered,

> The Methodists must take heed to their doctrine, their experience, their practice, and their discipline. If they attend to their doctrines only, they will make the people antinomians; if to the experimental part of religion only, they will make them enthusiasts; if to the practical part only, they will make them Pharisees; and if they do not attend to their discipline, they will be like persons who bestow much pains in cultivating their garden, and put no fence round it, to save it from the wild boar of the forest.[30]

In 1786 John Wesley declared,

---

[30]Davies, George, and Rupp, *History of the Methodist Church in Great Britain*, 4:194.

I am not afraid that the people called Methodists should ever cease to exist either in Europe or America. But I am afraid lest they should only exist as a dead sect, having the form of religion without the power. And this undoubtedly will be the case unless they hold fast both the doctrine, spirit, and discipline with which they first set out.[31]

We affirm the sacraments of baptism and communion as means of grace.

A *sacrament* is an outward and visible sign of an inward and spiritual grace given unto us. A sacrament has been instituted and ordained by Christ himself as a means by which we receive grace. This grace is not automatically imparted through the ritual. It is imparted by a faith in Christ which leads us to obey his command. The sacraments are God's pledge or seal to assure us that we have been forgiven, received the Spirit, and adopted into the family of God. We receive strength and confirmation through these sacraments. We hold the real presence of Christ at his table. He comes through his Spirit and is not confined to the physical elements or restricted to a prescribed liturgy.

Yet our emphasis is not on ritual, but on the reality of the new birth. There is no separated order of priests who perform sacerdotal ministries. W. B. Pope was emphatic that such a view of Christian ministry, which understands clergy as priests, dishonors the unique role of Jesus Christ as our only mediator. The Christian altar is the cross

---

[31]Wesley, *BE Works*, 9:527.

which is available to the entire church.[32] We affirm open communion as an acknowledgment that we are only part of the body of Christ.

We affirm Christian perfection as maturity in Christ and conformity to the character of Christ.

Classic Methodism was also characterized by its asserting that it is the believer's privilege to be delivered from indwelling sin in this life.

Sanctification begins when we are born again. We are set apart from the old life of sin. And we grow in sanctification as a believer. Discipleship is essentially progressive sanctification.

There is not a complete deliverance from the remains of sin in the new birth. *Entire* sanctification is *entire* in the same sense that total depravity is *total* inability. Thus, the cure goes as deep as the disease. Since sin has a two-fold nature, salvation also has a two-fold deliverance.

Entire sanctification is the condition of loving God with all our heart. This love expels all sin, cleansing the heart from all unrighteousness. This term corresponds with the term *Christian perfection*, but neither term implies the end of growth or progress.

All theological systems teach a doctrine of sanctification, but they disagree as to how much progress can be made. It has been reduced to a philosophy. For others it is a mystical or charismatic experience. In other cases it is a doctrinal proposition to be affirmed. It has also been presented as an ascetic state we arrive at through extra-biblical rules. It has also been taught as a condition that

---

[32]Pope, *Compendium*, 3:336-337.

occurs when we belong to a corporate organization. In still other emphases, it amounts to a private pietism.

Wesleyanism is pessimistic about man's nature, but optimistic about God's grace. "He who calls us is faithful and will do it" (1 Thess 5:24). God can save completely or to the uttermost (Heb 7:25). This phrase, *to the uttermost*, means salvation is to the farthest extent, to the greatest degree, to the most distant point. Full salvation is not only freedom from the guilt, the bondage, and the power of sin, but cleansing from the pollution and nature of sin and ultimately deliverance from the very presence of sin.

But how much of this complete salvation may be experienced in this life? "Now to him who is able to do immeasurably more than all we ask or imagine, according to his power that is at work with us" (Eph 3:20). "No limit is set on Christian privilege."[33] William Sangster argued that "no man has a right to put a limit on what the grace of God can do."[34] There is more grace available in this life than most theological systems allow. If God is sovereign, there is no limit to the grace he can extend. Albert Outler explained, "For Wesley, the doctrine of perfection was yet another way of celebrating the *sovereignty* of grace!"[35]

This sanctifying work of the Spirit occurs in all true believers, whether or not they embrace Wesleyan theology. While it is not necessary to adhere to a particular

---

[33]Platt, "Perfection," *Encyclopedia of Religion and Ethics*, 9:728.

[34]Sangster, "The Church's One Privation,"493-507.

[35]Outler, *John Wesley*, 253.

theological system to experience perfecting grace, it is the duty of the church to counsel, teach, and provide spiritual guidance for believers. The Wesleyan synthesis is the most adequate framework in which to diagnose spiritual needs, discern spiritual unbalance, and direct spiritual formation.

We affirm the expansion and triumph of God's kingdom through the preaching of the gospel and revival.

Classic Methodism held a covenant, not dispensational theology. We affirm five essential doctrines regarding the last days:

- The second advent. Jesus Christ will literally return a second time.
- The resurrection of all mankind from the dead
- The final judgment
- Everlasting heaven
- Everlasting hell

However, some people are obsessed with speculation and like to argue over the rapture, the great tribulation, Armageddon, the Antichrist, and the millennium. Methodism is willing for people to "think and let think" on such secondary issues. The emphasis of Methodist eschatology was the warning to "flee the wrath to come."[36]
As well, Methodism has always tended to be optimis-

---

[36]Wesley, "The Great Assize," Sermon #15.

tic about the spread of the gospel and the advancement of Christ's kingdom. Wesley declared,

> Give me one hundred preachers who fear nothing but sin and desire nothing but God, and I care not a straw whether they be clergy or laymen, such alone will shake the gates of hell and set up the kingdom of heaven upon earth.[37]

Rather than a pessimistic view which advocates retreat and hopes for rapture, we expect revival. John Wesley who preached,

> But shall we not see greater things than these? Yea, greater than have been yet from the beginning of the world? Can Satan cause the truth of God to fail? Or his promises to be of none effect? If not, the time will come when Christianity will prevail over all, and cover the earth. Let us stand a little, and survey this strange sight, a *Christian world*.[38]

Thus, the Methodist hope was "to reform the nation, and in particular the Church, to spread scriptural holiness over the land."[39] This would result in real Christians whose lives would provoke the Jews to jealousy. The conversion of the Jews would result in a still larger harvest among Muslims and the pagan world. Thus, the

---

[37]Wesley, *Letter* to Alexander Mather, 6 August 1777.

[38]Wesley, "Scriptural Christianity," 3.1.

[39]Wesley, *BE Works*, 10:845.

resurrection of the church would result in the millennium or a Christian world established on earth. The irony is that the American holiness movement reveres Daniel Steele who defended Methodist eschatology, but has adopted a dispensational theology of the last days.[40]

Now we will move from the predominant themes of classic Methodism to its classic literary expressions.

CLASSIC ENGLISH METHODIST LITERATURE

John Wesley (1703-1791)

The obvious starting point is the writings of John Wesley. John Wesley is a respected church leader and theologian in church history, but he is not infallible. As a godly scholar, his interpretations of the Scriptures are often accurate; but final authority resides in the Scriptures, not in Wesley. Some people, therefore, object to following any man. They claim to teach only what the Bible teaches, yet they sound very much like one or two of their favorite media preachers.

Despite his imperfections, Wesley was a master of logic. He also had a working knowledge of the early church fathers. As well he had a grasp of the original biblical languages. Then, after thirteen years as an ordained Anglican clergyman, he was convinced that he lacked saving faith and was born again!

Wesley represents a balance of scholarship and anointing. His preaching has been described as "logic on

---

[40]See Steele, *A Substitute for Holiness or Antinomianism Revived* and "Why I Am Not a Premillennialist."

fire." He was used mightily by God, but so were other men and women with whom Wesley disagreed. The best biography of Wesley is by Kenneth Collins, *A Real Christian* (1999).

His contribution to the church was his ability to synthesize early church tradition, Greek Orthodox, Roman Catholic, Lutheran, Calvinistic, the mystics, Puritan, and Anglican contributions to theology, through the grid of Scripture. Thus, Thomas Oden concluded that Wesleyan theology is a particular branch from the patristic tradition that is rooted in the ancient ecumenical teaching.[41]

Wesley never desired to create another sectarian division within the church and steadfastly refused to leave the Church of England. He upheld a catholic spirit, but contended for fundamental Christian doctrine — while advocating toleration for nonessential doctrines. He was not a pluralist, a latitudinarian, or a liberal, but he did "think and let think" — a phrase he often employed. As an organizational genius, he was pragmatic.

Methodism is a revival of apostolic Christianity, not as a sectarian point of view. It represents the best balance between a clear mind and a warm heart. John Wesley never wrote a systematic theology, but Oden argued that no major Christian doctrine is neglected in Wesley's teachings and that Wesley was a systematic theologian.[42]

William Carpenter edited a compendium of Wesley's doctrines in systematic order in a book called *Wesleyana*. It was reprinted by The Allegheny Wesleyan Methodist Connection, in 1979.

Robert W. Burtner and Robert E. Chiles did much the

---

[41]Oden, *John Wesley's Teachings*, 1:25.

[42]Oden, *John Wesley's Teachings*, 1:21-23.

same thing in *A Compend of Wesley's Theology* (1954),but drew from a wider source of Wesley material.

It may come as a surprise to learn that the Articles of Religion, Wesley's Standard Sermons, and his *Explanatory Notes Upon the New Testament* are all authoritative statements of doctrine in the United Methodist Church. This was reaffirmed as recently as the 1988 General Conference. The tragedy is that the UMC became apostate because its bishops refuse to enforce Methodist doctrine and practice.[43]

The Standard Sermons of Wesley

Every Bible-believing Methodist preacher should own Wesley's *Standard Sermons*. While there is an academic debate over whether there are forty-four or fifty-two standard sermons, the point is that Wesley intended some of his sermons to serve as a doctrinal standard for Methodism. Wesley never wrote a systematic theology, but his genius was that he provided model sermons for his lay preachers. This provision kept Methodism conservative until more recent times because it kept everyone on the same page.

Thomas Oden explained that these standard sermons and notes fulfill six functions:

1. The standards serve as an authoritative *guide* to one seeking the essential and central truth of Scripture.

---

[43]For the most thorough documentation of this dereliction of duty see Spann, *Conservatives in the Great Deep of the Methodist Church, 1900-1980.*

2. They serve as an authoritative *standard* to which appeal can be made in matters of controversy.

3. They serve as an authoritative *source* from which the truth is received.

4. They serve to *regulate* the teaching office of the church. Those ordained into Christian ministry ought to clearly understand essential Christian teachings.

5. They *unite* a diverse church body in a common doctrinal purpose.

6. They *defend* church property against abuses by those who would not hold these views.[44]

As you read these standard sermons, keep in mind that Wesley embellished these sermons with frequent illustrations. He was even criticized for telling too many stories.[45] However, he published his sermons without illustrations to give his lay preachers a basic outline from which to work. They were expected to supply their own illustrations. Wesley did not read his sermons; these written sermons were preparation for delivery and a means of reaching those who could not hear him preach orally.

Also remember that while the English language has changed since Wesley's day, he intended to be understood by the common people. As a young preacher he once read a sermon to a servant and got her to stop him whenever she did not understand. And so his language will have to be updated and his outlines will have to be

---

[44]Oden, *Doctrinal Standards in the Wesleyan Tradition*, 15, 21.

[45]Telford, *The Life of John Wesley*, 316.

adapted, but his doctrine does not need to be modernized.

Oden divides the standard sermons into six major themes:

1. The foundation: justification by grace through faith, sermons 1-5.
2. The assurance of the Spirit: faith taking root in the heart, sermons 6-20
3. Faith bearing fruit in the Christian life, sermons 21-36.
4. The spirit of peace, sermons 37-39.
5. The way of salvation, sermons 15, 43-48.
6. Christian perfection, sermons 40-42, 49-53.[46]

While the sermons are not arranged in an exact order, Steve Harper says #1-16 reflect the essence of salvation, #17-40 the order of salvation, #41-53 the application of salvation.[47] Kenneth Collins concludes the sermons contain little theoretical or speculative discussion. Basically they deal with two questions, how do I become a Christian and how do I remain one?[48]

These sermons corrected the shallow and unscriptural approach to evangelism in Wesley's day. Nathanael Burwash described the attack on evangelical doctrine by pointing out

the doctrine of faith, by what appeared to be a

---

[46]Oden, *Doctrinal Standards*, 94-97.

[47]Harper, "Wesley's Sermons as Spiritual Formation Documents," 133.

[48]Collins, *Wesley on Salvation*, 129-130.

very slight modification, but which was in reality a total perversion of its principles, was easily imitated by an antinomian theory of salvation by logical deduction. A commercial view of the atonement, a disregard of the profound work of the Spirit, and of the necessity of repentance, and a resting in an intellectual assurance instead of the God-given witness of the Spirit, these were the elements out of which was constructed an imitation of evangelical religion which, even in Mr. Wesley's day, threatened to pervert the great work of grace which God had wrought through his preaching.[49]

If you are buying only the standard sermons, keep in mind there are five annotated editions: W. P. Harrison (1886), Nathanael Burwash (1881), Edward H. Sugden (1921), Albert C. Outler, as part of the Bicentennial Edition 1984-1987, and most recently Kenneth J. Collins (2013). John Lawson's *Notes on Wesley's Forty-Four Sermons* (1946) contains commentary, but not the text of the sermons.

The Wesley Workbook, edited by Robert L. Brush and me in 1996 collected the best insights from the four annotated editions then in existence, as well as the essay by C. Leslie Mitton, *A Clue to Wesley's Sermons*, and a study guide.

---

[49]Burwash, *Wesley's Doctrinal Standards*, xvii.

Wesley's Explanatory Notes upon the New Testament

Scholars may find his New Testament notes disappointing because of their brevity. It was Wesley's practice to organize a Methodist society and start by reading and explaining the first chapter of Matthew. When he moved on, his notes were to serve as a guide as lay leaders continued the exposition chapter-by-chapter. They reflect an awareness of textual issues and theological controversies, but they are written at a lay level. They would be helpful for any Sunday School teacher.

It should be noted, however, that when Wesley came to the book of Revelation, he translated Johann Albrecht Bengel, a German Lutheran, without necessarily endorsing all that Bengel wrote. This was unfortunate since many people assume that these notes reflect Wesley's opinion. However, they were published with the disclaimer from Wesley, "Every part of this I do not undertake to defend."[50]

Bengel proposed an advent of Christ before the millennium as well as a third advent after the millennium. While this interpretation is not unique to Bengel, it is not a common interpretation. As one scholar explained, "Wesley did not commit himself to Bengel's views but merely put them forward for consideration."[51]

Wesley also wrote a three-volume commentary on the Old Testament. It was never considered to be as valuable as his notes on the New Testament, which exist in

---

[50]Wesley *Notes*, 4, 650.

[51]Wainwright, *Mysterious Apocalypse*, 79. See also Maddox, *Responsible Grace*, 236-239.

many formats. He relied upon Matthew Henry for his Old Testament notes, but stated openly that he had edited out all Henry's references to the doctrine of "absolute, irrespective, unconditional predestination."[52] There is a facsimile reprint of the *Explanatory Notes Upon the Old Testament* (1975), but they would be more beneficial to the scholar.

G. Roger Schoenhals edited a one-volume condensation of Wesley's notes on the Old and New Testament. It was originally published in 1987 under the title *Wesley's Notes on the Bible*. In 1990 Zondervan Publishing House reprinted this edition as *John Wesley's Commentary on the Bible*. It is out of print, but if you can find one it is worth having.

The Works of John Wesley

In 1872 Thomas Jackson edited a fourteen-volume set of the Works of John Wesley. This set contains his journal, his sermons, and his letters. If Wesley's journal was his accountability, and his sermons were his theology, then his letters were his spiritual counsel. This Jackson edition of Wesley's Works has been reprinted several times since 1959 and are relatively inexpensive. They contain 141 sermons, not just the standard sermons.

For scholars the new Bicentennial Edition, which was begun in 1975, now has 26 volumes in print. This includes 151 sermons, an annotated journal and letters, and essays. It contains fifteen new sermons by Wesley that were not included in the Jackson edition and it omits four sermons in the Jackson edition which were not actu-

---

[52]Wesley, *Notes*, 1:iv.

ally written by Wesley.

There are nine more volumes to be released making this a projected 35-volume set. Volumes 5-6 will contain Wesley's *Explanatory Notes Upon the New Testament*. This bicentennial edition is expensive and is probably necessary only for scholars.

The Christian Library edited by Wesley

At the time of his death, John Wesley had 294 lay preachers under his direction. His concern for these preachers included their reading. He told them to read the most useful books, and that regularly and constantly. For those who claimed to have no taste for reading, his advice was, "Contract a taste for it by use, or return to your trade." While that might sound harsh, his reply to those who had no books was very generous. "I will give each of you, as fast as you will read them, books up to the value of five pounds. "And I desire the assistants will take care that all the large Societies provide *The Christian Library* for the use of the preachers.[53] The largest single block of sources, more than a third, came from the Puritan tradition.[54]

The Christian Library was originally a fifty-volume set produced in 1749-1755. As he "extracted" the works of his favorite authors, he preserved roughly one page out of every fifty pages of original text. He was careful to edit out any hint of the doctrine of predestination and to emphasize what he judged was their most edifying contributions to the common thread of Christian piety. In 1819-

---

[53]Wesley, *BE Works*, 10:887-888.

[54]Monk, *John Wesley: His Puritan Heritage* (1966).

1826 a thirty-volume second edition was published.

John Fletcher (1729-1785)

Every Methodist should know the name John Fletcher. Jean Guillaume de la Fléchère was born in Nyon, Switzerland. For seven years he attended college and academy in Geneva, which had been the stronghold of John Calvin.

Fletcher moved to England around the age of twenty where he anglicized his name to John William Fletcher. John Wesley designated Fletcher to be his successor as the leader of the Methodist Church, but Fletcher died six years prior to Wesley's own death. Perhaps the greatest tribute to Fletcher was paid by Voltaire, the French infidel. When asked if he had ever met anyone like Jesus Christ, Voltaire lapsed into silence and then replied, "I once met Fletcher of Madeley."[55]

Fletcher pastored the Anglican congregation in Madeley for 25 years. Madeley was a mining town in Shropshire, England. Although he was offered a more affluent parish, Fletcher replied, "I want nothing but more grace."[56]

Like all of the early Methodists, Fletcher opposed Calvinism on the one hand and rational deism on the other hand. Fletcher is most famous for his *Checks to Antinomianism* and his *Portrait of St. Paul*. His five The *Checks* were written to vindicate Wesley against Calvin-

---

[55]Abbey and Overton, *English Church in the Eighteenth Century*, 2:113; see also Sangster, *Path to Perfection*, 32; *Pure in Heart*, 60.

[56]Benson, *Life of Fletcher*, 167.

ism. His *Portrait* was originally written in French, but only published in English. This book ends with a rebuttal of Voltaire and Rosseau, two of the rationalistic philosophers of that day.

The only reprint of Fletcher's writings in the twentieth century was the four-volume reprint by Schmul Publications in 1974. In secondary literature, the best introduction to Fletcher's theology is *True Christianity* by J. Russell Frazier (2014). I am told that there are approximately four hundred Fletcher sermon manuscripts in French and English that have never been translated and printed.

Adam Clarke (1762?-1832)

Adam Clarke was the great Methodist commentator. As a small boy in Northern Ireland, Adam repeatedly failed his lessons, even though his father was the schoolmaster. One day a visiting teacher came and examined some of the students. When he came to Adam, he was told, "That boy is slow at learning. I fear you will not be able to do much with him." But the visitor spoke kindly to Adam, laid his hand on his head and declared, "This lad will make a good scholar yet." Adam recalled that something had broken within him. This kindness gave hope to Adam and he found that he could commit his lessons to memory with ease.[57]

Adam went on to learn twenty languages, becoming the most able biblical scholar of his time. While Clarke never abandoned his pastoral ministries, he became a great scholar in classic literature, patristics, languages, history, geology, and natural science. When the Rosetta

[57]Tracy, *When Adam Clarke Preached*, 13-14.

Stone first arrived in England the Society of Antiquarians did not know what the third language was. It contained hieroglyphics, Greek, and an unknown third language. Clarke made a trip to their offices and identified the third language as Coptic.

His greatest work was his *Commentary* which took him twenty-five years to write and fifteen years to get published (1810-1826). Clarke said, "I wrote every page of it in reference to the ministers of the word of God, and especially those among the Methodists; and I know of no work, be it what it may, in which the doctrines of the Methodists are so clearly stated, illustrated, and proved."[58]

Clarke was a pioneer in the field of lower criticism, which today is called textual criticism. This is the comparison and evaluation of biblical manuscripts in order to determine the correct reading. This is in contrast to higher criticism, which is a liberal attempt to determine how the biblical text evolved through natural means. By definition, higher criticism dismisses divine inspiration. Clarke affirmed divine inspiration and biblical inerrancy.

The Abingdon reprint of Clarke's six-volume commentary, done in 1950 is out of print. They did a three-double-volume reprint in 1977, which is also out of print. However, Schmul Publishers has recently printed a superior edition.

Unfortunately, the one-volume abridgement by Ralph Earle in 1967 imposes a later American holiness misunderstanding of the book of Acts on Clarke's comments.[59]

Adam Clarke did not write a systematic theology, but

---

[58]Dunn, *Christian Theology*, 45.

[59]See my review, "The Earle and Clarke Exposition," 5-8.

his biographer Samuel Dunn went through Clarke's writings and compiled Clarke's *Christian Theology* in 1835. It is available through Schmul Publications.

They also reprinted *The Christian Prophet and His Work* by Adam Clarke. This 152-page book contains a sermon by that title, his *Clavis Biblica*, and his "Letter to a Preacher." Clarke wrote *Clavis Biblica* for two converted Buddhist priests who came to England to observe Christianity. A *clavis* is a key or glossary and this clavis is a summary of the Bible and its teachings.

Clarke said,

> No man ever taught me the doctrine I embraced; I received it singly by reading the Bible. From that alone I saw that justification by faith, the witness of the Spirit, and the sanctification of the heart were all attainable. These I saw as clearly as I do now; and from them I have never swerved. I often read the Bible on my knees. When I came to a passage I did not fully understand, I said, "Lord, here is thy book; it is given for the salvation of man; it can be no salvation to him unless he understand it; thou has the key of this text, unlock it to me;" and praying thus I generally received such light as was satisfactory to myself.[60]

However, this confidence led Clarke to eccentric interpretations on a few occasions. He opened the door to a firestorm of controversy with his comments on Luke 1:35. There he took the position that the term "Son of

---

[60]Etheridge, *Life of Clarke*, 358.

God" applies to Jesus Christ *after* the Incarnation. Fearful that this interpretation would open the door to rationalism, Richard Watson wrote *Remarks on the Eternal Sonship of Christ* in 1818.

By 1827 the Methodist Conference passed a resolution requiring every candidate for ordination to affirm the eternal sonship of Jesus Christ. Clarke never answered his critics, but continued to work on his commentary. The bottom line is that Clarke was not heretical, but the Methodist leadership was fearful that his interpretation could be exploited by those who were challenging the doctrine of the Trinity.

My analysis is that Watson thought as a systematic theologian, while Clarke thought as an exegete. The immediate result was that the Methodist Connection did not endorse Clarke's *Commentary*, but promoted Joseph Benson's five-volume *Notes* instead. However, Benson was not reprinted and over time Clarke's *Commentary* has received acclaim. Milton S. Terry wrote,

> Next to Matthew Henry's exposition no work of similar scope and magnitude has had a wider circulation or is better known than the commentary of Adam Clarke. It is marked by several eccentricities of opinion, but displays a vast amount of learning, and is a monument of the tireless industry of its author. It has especially served a useful purpose among the Methodist ministry and people, by whom it has been chiefly used.[61]

---

[61]Terry, *Biblical Hermeneutics*, 728.

Richard Watson (1781-1833)

The Watson family attended Calvinistic congregations while Richard was growing up. In his early teen years his father began attending a Methodist chapel. It grieved Richard that his family now mistakenly preferred Wesleyan theology to that of Calvin. He had been raised in church, but for a short time he fell into mischief and delighted in disrupting the Methodist services. Although he began reading Latin at six, Richard left grammar school after he was fourteen to become an apprentice carpenter. Then he was deeply convicted of sin. He was convinced that justification was through faith in the blood of Christ. Believing that Christ died as a sacrifice for his sins, he put his trust in Christ His midnight was turned into the light of day and guilt was replaced by love, The Holy Spirit bore a distinct and indubitable witness with his spirit that was a child of God.

He began preaching at fifteen. He had a sharp memory. If he read a work once, he retained most of it. It he read it twice, it was his. Yet Watson was conscious that he needed the anointing of the Spirit to preach effectively. For Watson preaching was serious business and he became increasingly partial to the expositional mode of preaching. He was regarded as an extraordinary preacher and often preached with unusual power.

At nineteen he wrote a pamphlet entitled, "An Apology for the Methodists" in which he defended Methodism from misrepresentation. Watson enjoyed taking the role of "devil's advocate" in doctrinal matters to sharpen his skills as a debater. However, he was misunderstood and fell under suspicion of heresy. Refusing to defend himself, he resigned the ministry in 1801. After his marriage, his father-in-law persuaded him to unite with a small society. Two and a half years later he reentered the ministry with the Methodist New Connection. By 1807 he was appointed their secretary.

In 1812 he returned to the original Methodist body through the influence of Jabez Bunting. He was active in the formation of the Wesleyan Missionary Society and served as its secretary for fourteen years. He was also involved in the opposition to slavery. On his death bed, he rejoiced in the news that the British Parliament was moving toward their emancipation in the West Indies.

In 1818 Watson wrote *Remarks on the Eternal Sonship of Christ* as a rebuttal to Clarke. Nothing he wrote brought him greater satisfaction than this pamphlet. When a biography of John Wesley by Robert Southey reduced Wesley's faith to philosophic principles, the Wesleyan book committee asked Watson to write a defense of Wesley.

At the conference of 1821 he was relieved of pastoral duties so that he might oversee the work of missions and write. Eighteen months later the first section of his *Theological Institutes* was published. Thomas Jackson wrote that "on all doctrinal questions an absolute deference is paid to the authority of Scripture." The final section was completed in 1829.

Jackson noted that the sentences were sometimes too long and involved. However, it was the first Methodist systematic theology and became a standard text in 1825 — even before the last section was completed. It remained on the Course of Study for half a century. American Methodist theologians such as Thomas Ralston, Luther Lee, Samuel Wakefield, and Amos Binney, were imitations of Watson's *Institutes*. Robert Chiles wrote,

"Both in Britain and in America Richard Watson was easily the single most determinative of the early Methodist theologians."[62] The *Institutes* was reprinted by Lexham Press in 2018 with a new introduction by Ben Witherington III.

On his deathbed he stated, "The Methodists have right views of the atonement; and they also know the way of coming to the atonement, and the right use to be made of that important doctrine." Everything he uttered centered on the atonement. He repeatedly declared, "The atonement is the sinner's short way to God. On this rock I rest, and feel it firm beneath me."[63]

Before his untimely death at age fifty-two, Watson wrote also wrote a biblical and theological dictionary. In his abridged dictionary, printed by Fundamental Wesleyan Publishers in 2000, Watson addresses philosophical issues, comparative religions, apologetics, matters of hermeneutics, and basic Christian beliefs. The chief value of this dictionary is its refutation of Calvinism. Whoever defines the terms, controls the debate. Watson's definitions and historical accounts, his exegesis and citation of primary sources will strengthen this generation of ill-equipped Arminians to defend their faith.

Watson rejected the rationalism formulated in German schools. He affirmed the full authority and inerrancy of Scripture. He held that it was legitimate to use reason in sorting out textual variants and in interpreting the meaning of the text, but once the text was established and understood — revelation takes priority over reason. Regarding the assurance of personal salvation, Watson

---

[62] Chiles, *Theological Transition,* 42.

[63] Jackson, *Life of Watson*, 442.

clearly embraces the doctrine of the direct witness of the Spirit.

Watson held that Genesis 1-3 was to be accepted as a literal account and that the flood was universal. While his article on Arianism might wrongly be thought obsolete, it works just as well against Jehovah's Witnesses as it did against Arians. Watson had an adequate grasp of the Trinity and dealt with early church heresies concerning the nature of Christ.

Watson contended for the virgin birth of Christ and dealt extensively with the atonement. In addition to all this, he included articles on expiation, propitiation, and sacrifice. As previously mentioned, Watson is most helpful in his analysis of Calvinism. Included is a fifteen-page account of the Synod of Dort which shows the intolerance and injustice with which Arminians were treated. Watson's definitions of terms such as: calling, election, foreknowledge, necessity, predestination, reprobation, will, and vocation are Arminian.

Watson rejected such doctrines as universalism and annihilationism, which have been embraced by some liberal Arminians of our day. Watson's vigorous denunciation of Roman Catholicism reflects the view of the Reformers. While holding to a historical approach to the interpretation of prophetic passages, Watson's greatest strength regarding eschatology is his optimism that the kingdom of Christ will prevail.

William Burt Pope (1822-1903)

In 1809 three Methodist preachers went to Plymouth in England and a revival broke out in the nearby village of Turnchapel. A Methodist society was organized from five young men who were converted there. Eventually, all of them became preachers or missionaries. John Pope eventually moved to Nova Scotia, where his son William Burt was born on February 19, 1822. Later that year the family moved to the West Indies as missionaries.

When John's brother died, the family had to move to England in 1826 to manage his estate. W. B. was educated in England under John Hannah. Pope would later edit Hannah's theological lectures for publication as an act of loyalty and generosity.

Pope entered the Methodist ministry in 1841 and taught at Didsbury Wesleyan College in Manchester from 1867-1886. He was elected president of the Bristol Methodist Conference in 1877. W. B. Pope "stands out as one of the towering figures in all of Methodist theology who with remarkable fidelity recaptured the essence of Wesley's theology," according to Robert E. Chiles.[64]

He was described as shy and retiring. His daily schedule set aside two hours for Hebrew, Greek, and Latin, three hours for theological study, and one hour for mathematics, with German, history, and biography filling in discretionary time.

From 1860-1879 Pope translated commentaries and other theological works for the T. and T. Clark Theological Library from conservative, evangelical German theologians who upheld supernatural revelation against the Tubingen school of rationalists.

Then from 1875-1876 he produced his greatest work, the three-volume *A Compendium of Christian Theology*, after first publishing *Introductory Lectures on the Study of Christian Theology*, by his tutor, John Hannah (1872).

---

[64]Chiles, *Theological Transition*, 34.

Thomas Langford wrote,

> There is little in the *Compendium* that differs
> from Wesley, Clarke, or Watson. The same is-
> sues are discussed and similar conclusions are
> reached. The distinctive quality of Pope's writ-
> ing lay in his style of expression, his lucidity,
> and his completeness. He carried out the Wes-
> leyan emphases and his chief contribution was
> perhaps his continuation of the doctrine of the
> universal range of God's gracious redemptive
> activity, which is free in all, to all, and for all.[65]

Yet his biographer, R. W. Moss described Pope as
one whose intellectual sympathies were mainly with the
past. Pope was not impressed with Charles Darwin nor in
the higher criticism which applied evolutionary theory to
the development of Scripture.

Pope became the dominant figure in Methodist theology and, next to John Wesley himself, did more to provide Methodism with a systematic standard of doctrine
than anyone else. He grasped and elucidated the grace of
God as the key to Wesleyan theology. He respected the
genuine freedom of man without shifting the emphasis
from grace to free will. It is this concept of grace which
enabled Methodism to avoid both Pelagianism and Calvinistic predestinarianism. In William Burt Pope the spirit
of John Wesley's theology lived again. Pope "ruled as a
sun over the day," but with his passing "the voices of the
night" began to call to each other. In particular, these
"voices" were advocating biblical higher criticism, ratio-

---

[65]Langford, *Practical Divinity*, 69.

nalism, ecumenicism, evolution, and social liberalism.[66]

Pope declared that Methodism "preached the testimony of the Holy Ghost in the heart of the believer as the common prerogative; and further, the attainableness in this life of a state of entire sanctification and acceptableness in the sight of God."[67] It was also reported that during the communion services he led, the spiritual power was sometimes almost overwhelming. Men not easily moved broke down and sobbed aloud. "Dr. Pope taught his men theology, but he led them also into the very presence of God."[68]

Fred Sanders, a systematic theologian at Biola University, found a dilapidated set of Pope's *Compendium* at a used book store and bought them "to see what this fellow was all about." Sanders said that before he was very far into the first volume Pope had made his head spin. He declared that Pope handled theological themes as if they were holy things. He listed it as one of his top ten ranked books.[69] On another website he has asked to finish this sentence, "You haven't really considered Wesleyanism unless you've read . . ." Sanders then referenced Pope and said, "I think is one of the finest theological minds in Protestant history, sadly neglected."[70]

The irony is that while Pope is commonly described as the prince of Wesleyan theologians, nothing he wrote

---

[66]Dunlap, "Methodist Theology in Great Britain," 425.

[67]Pope, *Peculiarities of Methodism*, 11-13.

[68]Moss, *Pope: Theologian and Saint,* 90.

[69]Sanders, "Mind of William Burt Pope."

[70]Strand, "Strands of Thought."

is in print except for the Schmul reprint of *The Prayers of St. Paul* (2024). Recently, Justus Hunter has advocated a return to W. B. Pope. Hunter concluded

> His project carefully balances that which is peculiar with that which is shared by the broad stream of catholic evangelical truth, and in so doing produces a distinctively and provocatively Methodist theology. He is a Methodist mind caught up in the joy of faith's pursuit of understanding. We ought not continue to let him rest.[71]

Moss said he stood as a theologian at the parting of the ways. While Pope wrote the greatest exposition of Wesleyan doctrine, it came at a time when Methodism was departing from Wesley.

Here is a bibliography of Dr. Pope's major works:

1863. *Discourses on the Kingdom and Reign of Christ*
1871. *Discourse on the Person of Christ*
1875. *A Compendium of Christian Theology*
1876. *Memoir of the Late James Heald*
1876. *The Prayers of St. Paul*
1878. *Sermons, Addresses, and Charges*
1880. *Discourses on the Lordship of the Incarnate Redeemer*
1883. *Commentary on 1-3 John* in *A Popular Commentary on the New Testament*, Philip Schaff, ed.
1884. *A Higher Catechism of Theology*
1884. *Commentary on Ezra and Nehemiah* in *Ellicott's*

---

[71]Hunter, "Defense of William Burt Pope," 17/

Commentary on the Whole Bible
1885. *The Inward Witness*

Pope lived another eighteen years after his final book. His final years were wretched years of mental depression during which he took slight interest in passing events and found little consolation in either friends or books.

He had nine children. He lost two of them in infancy and never got over it. The sight of a winding funeral was unbearable and any death in the circle of his friends re-opened the sore. Every sunset was apt to bring pain.

By mid-life some of these tendencies had begun to surface. On occasions when he traveled he was overcome with a sense of loneliness that lingered for weeks afterward. This feeling tended to master him increasingly. At sixty-three he tried short periods of rest as he neared a breakdown. During these periods of rest he instructed a neighbor who looked after him not to talk of books or sermons. He found relief in observing nature. The depression, encouraged by predisposition and bodily sickness, continued to deepen and thus he retired from active ministry the following year. The rest of his life was spent in quiet seclusion.

His biographer also referred to tendencies which had been inherited and physical disease which did not yield to treatment. He was a shy man and subject to feelings of loneliness. Eventually he lost hold of reality in unbroken spiritual gloom and he retired at sixty-four from active service as a professor of theology.

None of his old haunts knew him any more; intercourse with his friends was avoided, and the solace of books failed him. He took a slight interest in the passing events of the day, and would at times send messages of greeting. To the pages of a small Greek Testament he turned now and again with symptoms of aspiration, if not of relief; but around his soul was drawn a thick curtain, through which no man was allowed to pass, and above his head the light was covered with clouds.[72]

While this seems like such a troubling description of such a great theologian, the fact is that we are all earthen vessels (2 Cor 4:7).

Lesser Known English Methodist Systematic Theologies

• John Locke, *A System of Theology* (1862). John Locke (1814-1890) of the Wesleyan Methodist Connection of Great Britain is not to be confused with the much more famous John Locke, the seventeenth century Enlightenment philosopher.

• William Cooke, *Christian Theology: its Doctrines and Ordinances Explained and Defended.* (1863). This is perhaps the first and only systematic textbook produced by the Methodist New Connection, a break away from the Wesleyan Connection of Great Britain, which demanded more rights and powers for the laity.

---

[72]Moss, *Pope: Theologian and Saint*, 122.

- Benjamin Field, *The Student's Handbook of Christian Theology* (1870). Field was a theologian in the Wesleyan Methodist Connection of Great Britain and died in Australia. This was reprinted in 1957. However, the section on eschatology was rewritten by Henry Shilling of Transylvania Bible School to reflect their premillennial position.

- John Hannah, *Introductory Lectures on the Study of Christian Theology: With Outlines of Lectures on the Doctrines of Christianity* (1872). This incomplete and unfinished work was written by Dr. Hannah, William Burt Pope's predecessor and mentor.

- Henry W. Williams, *A Manual of Natural and Revealed Theology, Designed Especially for Local Preachers, and Sunday-School Teachers* (1882). This work is a shortened and simplified systematic theology textbook. Williams based it on William Burt Pope's first edition work.

- John S. Banks, *A Manual of Christian Doctrine* (1902). He opposed the modernist theologies of his day

- Nathanael Burwash, *Manual of Christian Theology on the Inductive Method* (1900). As the leading Canadian Methodist, Burwash explained, "A man can be a Methodist today and believe far differently from what Methodists believed half a century ago."[73]

Joseph Agar Beet wrote *A Manual of Theology* in 1906 which accepted the findings of biblical criticism without hesitation. Beet was a Methodist scholar who generally reflected orthodox Methodist doctrine. However, he rejected the immortality of the soul and was noncommittal regarding final punishment.[74] At the turn of the twentieth century there was still enough residual orthodoxy left in mainline Methodism that Beet's heretical view on this issue was not generally accepted. Methodist theologian, John S. Banks, wrote a response to Beet's book on the immortality of the soul, entitled *Words of Immortality* (1902).

In his letter to the young ministers of the Methodist connexion, Pope explained that the advocates of this new doctrine claimed that immortality is conditional life in Christ. Pope advised these younger men to track the Greek words in a concordance. "The result will show that neither is life in Christ mere existence, nor death out of Christ annihilation." Pope advised the younger men to close their ears to eloquent preachers in high places who cannot support their views from solid exegesis of Scripture.[75] Sadly, Beet's position is cited both in Seventh Day

---

[73]See Van Die, *An Evangelical Mind* for the dismal results of Burwash's attempt to "update piety." His compartmentalized thinking affirmed classic Methodism *and* contemporary liberalism.

[74]Carter, "Joseph Agar Beet and the Eschatological Crisis," 197-216.

[75]Pope, "Letter to the Younger Ministers," 393-397.

Adventist and Jehovah's Witness literature as proof that they are right.

Wesley's Veterans

The stories of Old Testament saints and sinners were written for our example (1 Cor 10:6, 11). It is encouraging to watch God's providence at work in the unfolding of a good biography. In *The Tapestry* Edith Schaeffer wrote, "The thing that fascinates me really is the weaving of lives together, the fabulous way God works in history, while at the same time people's choices change history, for good or bad."[76]

In 1779 John Wesley requested that each of the itinerant Methodist preachers write an "account of the more remarkable circumstances of his life." Most of their autobiographies were printed in *The Arminian Magazine*. Then in 1837-1838 Thomas Jackson collected 36 of them into three volumes entitled, *Lives of Early Methodist Preachers*. This collection went through three editions and then was reprinted in 1914 as *Wesley's Veterans*. In 1976 Schmul Publishers reprinted them.

Wesley found working men who had spiritual gifts and an eagerness to serve and put them to work for the kingdom of God, giving them significant responsibilities and leadership. Abel Stevens wrote,

> The itinerants were taught to manage difficulties in the societies, to face mobs, to brave any weather, to subsist without means, except such as might casually occur on their routes, to rise at

---

[76]Schaeffer, *The Tapestry*, 13.

four and preach at five o'clock, to scatter books and tracts, to live by rule, and to die without fear.[77]

The longest autobiographies are those of John Nelson and Thomas Walsh. Both run almost two hundred pages, while the two shortest sketches run only eight pages. The average length is almost 50 pages. The beauty of such a collection is the variety of men God used and the variety of their experiences. Each testimony is unique. It would be impossible to decide which experience to seek. Instead, we begin to see the richness of God's grace. Many were saved from deep sin and were ignorant of spiritual matters. Other men had a good education and an early exposure to religion. They spoke honestly about their temptations and spiritual struggles. Their conversions were not superficial. Many also gave their testimony to having experienced entire sanctification.

Some of these lay preachers were mobbed while preaching in the open air. Many of their persecutors either died untimely deaths or were converted. These were men who lived and died well. Their accounts make challenging devotional reading.

Lesser Known English Methodist Writers

Edward Hare (1774-1818), was converted as a sailor and was taken prisoner twice during war with the French. He was later described as one of Methodism's most capable apologists, defended classic Methodist doctrine on such subjects as the atonement, the eternal Sonship of

---

[77]Stevens, *Illustrated History of Methodism*, 2:192-193.

Christ, justification, assurance, and against Socinianism and antinomianism. I demonstrated the significance of his defense of the Methodist doctrine of assurance in "Assurance or Presumption."[78]

Hare defended the Methodist doctrine of the inspiration of Scripture. He defined it as the Holy Spirit superintending the process so that the written record, faithfully recorded, is infallible.[79]

Richard Treffry wrote *A Treatise on Christian Perfection* in 1797. His son Richard Treffry, Jr. wrote *An Inquiry into the Eternal Sonship of Our Lord Jesus Christ* in 1837, *Letters on the Atonement* and *Lectures on Evidences of Christianity* in 1839.

Joseph Sutcliffe also published *The Doctrines of Justification by Faith, of Regeneration, of Assurance, and of Present Salvation* in 1806. He produced a catechism in the same year.

It is significant that classic Methodist doctrine was not articulated and defended by intellectual elitists, but by rank and file preachers of the gospel.

CLASSIC AMERICAN METHODIST LITERATURE

Francis Asbury and the Circuit Riders

John Wesley sent Francis Asbury to America in 1771. However, the growth of Methodism in America

---

[78]Reasoner, "Assurance or Presumption," 103-119.

[79]Hare, *The Principle Doctrines of Christianity*, 238, 257, 379.

was slowed down by the Revolutionary War. After the war, the Methodist Episcopal Church organized in 1784, where Asbury was also ordained a bishop. Asbury was a bishop on horseback. For forty-one years he traveled six thousand miles per year — totaling over a quarter of a million miles. He preached 16,500 sermons and ordained four thousand preachers. He became a legend. A friend in England once mailed him a letter addressed, "The Reverend Bishop Asbury, North America" and it was delivered promptly. The largest annual salary he ever received was $80.

Francis Asbury (1745-1816) was frequently named as an editor for Methodist disciplines, minutes, and hymnals due to his role as bishop. However, he only wrote one book, *The Causes, Evils, and Cures of Heart and Church Divisions* in 1792. Grieved over the division instigated by James O'Kelly, Asbury extracted from the works of two Puritans, Jeremiah Burrough and Richard Baxter. The Schmul reprint of 2022 contains a new introduction by John N. Oswalt. The journal and letters of Asbury were reprinted in three volumes in 1958.

The Methodist Church started in 1784 with 104 circuit riders. This was the itinerant or circuit ministry. By 1881 there were over 16,000 itinerant ministers and close to four million members. The secret to the rapid growth was that Methodism kept moving. As the young country moved westward, the Methodist circuit riders kept on the move. They lived in primitive conditions. An old expression was, "the weather is so bad no one out today but crows and Methodist preachers."

Of the first 737 Methodist circuit riders, 203 died between the ages of 25-35 and 121 between the ages of 35-45. Two-thirds died before they could serve twelve years. Almost a third died within the first five years of ministry. The average life expectancy of a circuit rider was thirty-three years of age.

The itinerant ministry was a temporary method which required celibacy. If a circuit rider married, he had to "locate." Asbury once exclaimed, "I believe the devil and the women will get my preachers!"[80] By 1816, when Asbury died, celibacy was on its way out. Yet during the circuit rider era candidates for the ministry were asked four questions:

- Is this man truly converted?
- Does he know and keep our rules?
- Can he preach acceptably?
- Has he a horse?

A man on the east coast had finally had more Methodist preachers than he could stand. They had converted his wife and daughter, and they were working on him. He was tired of it, so he packed his wife, daughter, and their belongings on a wagon and headed west. After a year on the road and across prairies when the road ended, he thought he was about ready to begin a new household. That evening while he was considering setting up his home where he camped, a young Methodist circuit rider, Richmond Nolley, rode up to their campfire and introduced himself. The man's anger was something to see. "I left the east to get away from you Methodists, and you are here also. Isn't there anywhere we can go to escape?" The circuit rider laughed. "I'm sorry my friend, but even if you were to go to heaven or hell, there would be a Meth-

---

[80]Rudolf, *Francis Asbury*, 107.

odist preacher there first!"[81]

Methodism emphasized supernatural conversion, but also valued education. Circuit riders in America are often depicted with a book in hand. Religious tracts and books carried on horseback were the vital seeds of church planting.

Sections of Adam Clarke's *Commentary* were carried in the saddlebags, and at night the circuit riders would read and study his exposition of Scripture by firelight. They also frequently read Wesley's sermons and journals. According to Cartwright, when a circuit rider felt that God had called him to preach, instead of hunting up a college or biblical institute, he hunted up a hardy pony, some traveling apparatus, and a library comprised of the Bible, hymn book, and discipline. With a text that never wore out, he preached, "Behold the Lamb of God, that taketh away the sin of the world!"[82]

Peter Cartwright (1785-1872)

Cartwright was the quintessential circuit rider. Although the circuit rider method was dying out during his lifetime, Cartwright was a circuit rider for twenty years. He was groomed by Bishops Asbury and William McKendree and he preached in Kentucky, Tennessee, Ohio, Indiana, and Illinois.

Cartwright was converted at a camp meeting in 1801 and joined the Methodist Church. His autobiography was first published in 1856 and is still in print, the *Autobiography of Peter Cartwright*. In it he gives an eyewitness

---

[81]Rupp and Minnick. "Has He a Horse?" 16-19.

[82]Cartwright, *Autobiography*, 164.

account of the camp meeting. The great Cane Ridge camp meeting began in Kentucky as an interdenominational effort between Baptists, Methodists, Presbyterians. From this movement the Christian Church was organized.

The Presbyterians soon abandoned the camp method because it was too hard to control. However, Asbury felt it had potential. With great frontier crowds of thousands, the Methodist preachers had to guard against false doctrine, such as the Shakers, universalists, anti-Trinitarians, and Calvinists who would attempt to infiltrate the camp. Cartwright was also willing to debate Baptists and their "water-mocassin god" of immersion, whenever they infiltrated the camp to proselyte Methodist converts. The Methodists also had to control "rowdies," those who would attempt to sell liquor outside the camp ground, and emotional excess, such as getting the jerks.

It took a rugged masculine leader to maintain order. Cartwright was famous for his willingness to thrash anyone who would attempt to disrupt the services. On one occasion, Cartwright had just entered the pulpit and was reading his text when he looked up and saw General Andrew Jackson taking his seat. Someone on the platform pulled Cartwright's suit coat and whispered, "General Jackson has come in." Cartwright was indignant and responded audibly, "Who is General Jackson? If he don't get his soul converted, God will damn him as quick as he would a Guinea Negro!" The next day Jackson caught up with Cartwright and expressed his admiration. "If I had a few thousand such independent, fearless officers as you were, and a well-drilled army, I could take old England."[83]

---

[83]Cartwright, *Autobiography,* 133-134.

In 1826 Cartwright learned that there were those who were trying to make Illinois a slave state and so he decided to run for office. He was elected twice to the legislature and reported that he found a great deal of corruption in the legislature. In his last attempt in politics he ran for Congress, but was defeated by Abraham Lincoln.

Cartwright devoted an entire chapter to his encounters with early Mormons. Although they spare no effort today to appear mainstream Christian, this autobiography is a primary source which demonstrates what cut-throats they were. Cartwright reported after one conversation he had with Joseph Smith that he was "a very illiterate and impudent desperado in morals, but at the same time, he had a vast fund of low cunning."

Cartwright was a Methodist presiding elder (district superintendent) for fifty years. During that time he saw great change come to our nation. Toward the end of his life, Cartwright became a great advocate for Christian colleges. He once wrote that he often wondered whether he had done more good as a preacher or by distributing religious books.

American Methodist Theologians

Nathan Bangs (1778-1862)

Rather than merely rely on John Fletcher, who had refuted the old Calvinism, it was Nathan Bangs who first used the term *gracious ability* in his rebuttal of the New England Calvinism, but he also affirmed *moral inability*.[84]

---

[84]Scott, "Methodist Theology in America," 49-50, 114.

Bishop Bangs also opposed the teachings of Phoebe Palmer as "unsound, unscriptural, anti-Wesleyan and no doubt in many cases had caused deception."[85] Yet it is the opinion of Timothy Smith that by 1867, "her views had won out" in the American holiness movement.[86] He wrote *The Necessity, Nature, and Fruits of Sanctification* in 1851.

Amos Binney (1802-1878)

In 1840 Amos Binney published a brief *Theological Compend*, which was aimed at use by families and Sunday schools. This was revised in 1875 by Binney's son-in-law, Daniel Steele, and the revised edition is still in print.

Thomas Ralston (1806-1891)

The first American Methodist to write a systematic theology was Thomas N. Ralston. *Elements of Divinity* was first published in 1847. In 1871 a new edition more than doubled the number of pages, with help from the editor, Thomas Summers. Schmul reprinted this in 1971 and you may be able to find a used copy.

Samuel Wakefield (1799-1895)

The first *major* American Methodist systematic the-

---

[85]Stevens, *Life and Times of Nathan Bangs*, 396-402. I included this section as an appendix to the reprint of Stackpole, *The Evidence of Salvation*.

[86]Smith, *Revivalism and Social Reform*, 125.

ology, *A Complete System of Christian Theology* was published by Samuel Wakefield in 1869. I played a small part in getting it reprinted in 1985, acting as a middle-man for a member of my congregation who put up the money. Harold Schmul took the funding and published Wakefield. Essentially, each of these theologies were a simplification and adaptation of Richard Watson's *Theological Institutes.*

Miner Raymond (1811-1897)

Miner Raymond's three-volume *Systematic Theology* (1877-1879) was the first original American Methodist theology. According to Albert C. Knudson, at Boston School of Theology, the writings of such men as Miner Raymond were "obsolete before they ever came off the press."[87] This statement reflects the liberal bias of Knudson that Methodist theology must be based on academically correct philosophy rather than biblical authority.

Thomas O. Summers (1812-1882)

Summers was born in England. His father died when he was a year old. After his mother died, when he was six, he was raised by his grandmother until her death when he was seven. He was then raised by a great-aunt who was a stanch Calvinist. However, he sometimes slipped off to visit the Methodist chapel, which displeased her greatly. She died when he was sixteen. He immigrated to the United States in 1830.

---

[87]Knudson,"Henry Clay Sheldon," 179.

He rejected Calvinism and for a while struggled with unbelief. He frequently heard Methodist sermons, but they did not discuss the questions which agitated his mind. He consulted Calvinistic ministers, but they told him that the counsel of God was a mysterious secret. He would play the devil's advocate among the Methodists, taking the Calvinistic position. On one occasion a Methodist lady gave him a copy of Clarke's commentary on Romans. As he read Clarke's comments on Romans 8-9 he was transported with joy. He had found the key which opened the mysteries of the Bible and it was a new book to him.

He began to attend the Methodist class meetings regularly and began seeking God for the new birth. On January 16, 1833 he was born again. There was great rejoicing in the class meeting when he testified to his experience. His class leader judged that the Lord had a work for him to do. A year later the class leader told Thomas that he believed from that time Thomas had started attending the society that God would call him into ministry. Soon after that Thomas was granted a license to preach at the quarterly conference, which recommended that he be admitted on trial to the annual conference.

In 1855 Dr. Summers moved to Nashville to become the editor of the Southern Methodist Publishing House. In 1872 he found his office, library, journal, and unpublished manuscripts all in ashes when the northern army passed through Nashville and burned the publishing house. He wrote in his diary, "The Lord would not have permitted so great a calamity to happen to me, if he had not intended to overrule it for good; so I submit without murmuring."

While continuing as editor, in 1874 he began part-time service as Professor of Systematic Theology at Vanderbilt University. Vanderbilt was a newly established university in Nashville which was started as a Methodist institution. By 1878, he became Dean of the Biblical Department there.

It was reported that Summers knew the Articles of Religion, Wesley, Watson, and Fletcher by heart. Anything not in line with classical Wesleyanism was instantly picked up by his editorial eye. His biographer reported, "Where the truth was involved, he knew no man after the flesh. Truth was dearer to him than friendship, and if occasion had called for it he would have stood for it against the world."[88] Yet he possessed a good sense of humor and was loved by all denominations. He had a catholic spirit. He occasionally preached for Baptist and Presbyterian congregations in Nashville and they delighted in his ministry. Yet it was reported that they had to endure some good-natured ribbing about immersion and predestination.

As his life drew to a close, he spoke frequently about heaven. Shortly before his death, he feebly ascended the pulpit at First Baptist Church in East Nashville. He leaned on the pulpit and discoursed on the city of God in a way that melted every heart. A lady recalled, "We all cried and felt an indescribable awe as the old Doctor stood there before us looking so pale and so feeble, and talked so sweetly and longingly of heaven."

When the General Conference met in 1882, he was once again elected as secretary. He did well the first day, then left the conference slipping into a side room. There he lingered. As he heard the songs of Zion sung from the

---

[88]Fitzgerald, *Dr. Summers*, 212.

conference, he rallied, half lifted his hands and spoke these final words: "Faith, faith, faith!"[89]

Dr. Summers wrote commentaries on the four Gospels, Acts, and Romans, as well as a spate of other books. His 2-volume, *Systematic Theology*, published in 1888 after his death, is essentially a commentary on the Methodist Articles of Religion. I particularly value his treatment of the atonement in Book 1, Part 3, chapters 1-6.

Luther Lee (1800-1889)

Lee was a theologian in the Methodist Episcopal Church. He left the denomination over slavery and became a forefather of what would later become the Wesleyan Church. After the abolition of slavery, Lee returned and died a member of the Methodist Episcopal Church. He wrote *Elements of Theology, or An Exposition of the Divine Origin, Doctrines, Morals, and Institutions of Christianity* (1856).

John Miley (1813-1895)

By this time John Miley had published *The Atonement in Christ* (1879), which advocated the governmental view of the atonement which had been developed much earlier by Hugo Grotius. Summers refutes this view in favor of penal substitution.

However, Miley went on to publish his *Systematic Theology* (1893). It marked a turning point in Methodist theology away from original Methodist doctrine. Miley argued, "If God is a moral ruler over responsible subjects,

---

[89]Fitzgerald, *Dr.Summers*, 352.

they must be morally free." Thus, he argued that such subjects did not need preliminary grace, but could choose the good by virtue of their natural ability.[90]

Robert Chiles wrote *Theological Transition in American Methodism*, in which he compared the theology of Richard Watson with that of John Miley. Chiles calls this transition "from free grace to free will." Miley's theology was last reprinted in 1989. Unfortunately, Summer's theology was never reprinted.

R. S. Foster (1820-1903)

Foster was a prominent bishop in the Methodist Episcopal Church between 1872-1903 who wrote six volumes on particular topics in theology between 1889-1899. However he denied the literal resurrection of the body in *Beyond the Grave* (1879). This led to charges of heresy and that he had embraced a type of gnosticism.

Theological Drift

With the emphasis by Miley on free will and human reason, Methodist theology began to drift from biblical authority. However, the Methodist theological tradition was still reflected in spots. Milton S. Terry, who succeeded Raymond as chair of Christian Doctrine at Garrett Biblical Institute, epitomized the liberal transition. Much like Burwash, Terry believed that modern liberalism could be assimilated without any harm to the Christian message. While Terry attempted to portray himself as a "moderate," by 1926 every Methodist seminary in Amer-

---

[90]Miley, *Systematic Theology*, 2:274, 280.

ica had declared their orientation as "modernist."

The draft continued with Olin Curtis and Henry Sheldon, both students of Borden Parker Bowne. Bowne was associated with a philosophy called "personalism," which predominated Boston University, whose School of Religion is Methodism's oldest seminary. According to this view, truth is discovered through a person's self-conscious apprehension of himself. Bowne himself "discovered" that God is equally present and equally near in every event, but does not intervene miraculously.

Terry's successor at Garrett Biblical Institute was Harris Franklin Rall (1870-1964). Rall denied the infallibility of the New Testament writers, the corruption of human nature, and the deity of Christ. Therefore, the period of classic Methodist theologians ended. Institutional Methodism has since moved from personalism, to existentialism, to process theology.

E. M. Bounds (1835-1913)

Edward McKendree Bounds was born in Missouri. Before he was nineteen he had passed the bar and was licensed to practice as an attorney at law. In 1859 the young lawyer experienced entire sanctification and a call to full-time ministry. A few months later he took down his shingle and closed his law office. He began to devour the Bible and John Wesley's sermons. Before Christmas of 1859 he was preaching in a little Methodist Episcopal Church, South in Monticello, Missouri. In February of the following year he was licensed to preach.

Sometime during the fall of 1861 he was arrested by Union troops because of his denominational affiliation. The evidence is that he was treated harshly and placed in a federal prison at St. Louis. He began to function as a Confederate chaplain among the troops there. He was freed at the end of 1862 in a prisoner of war exchange. He continued to serve as a Confederate chaplain through the rest of the Civil War. Once more he was taken prisoner in November 1864.

After the war he pastored in Franklin, Tennessee and then in Selma, Alabama. While in Selma he met his future wife. In 1874 he was transferred to St. Louis and married her in 1876. She died in 1886, leaving him with three young children. Before her death, she requested that he marry her cousin, whom she was confident would make her husband a good wife and her children a good mother. Almost two years later, he married the woman his wife had chosen for him. She bore him three sons and a daughter. However, during that five-year period between 1886-1891 he had buried a wife and two young sons. Later in life Bounds also had two grown children who quietly rebelled by denying his faith and becoming agnostics.

The family moved to Nashville so that Bounds could become the associate editor of the official denominational paper of the Methodist Episcopal Church, South. He withstood every introduction of liberalism within his denomination, maintaining that the Bible was written "directly under the superintendency of the Holy Spirit." He declared, "We hold definitely without compromise in the last to the plenary inspiration of the Scriptures." [91]

In 1894 he resigned this position to become an evangelist. Birmingham Southern College, a Methodist institution in Alabama awarded him an honorary Doctor of Divinity degree for his faithful service as a preacher and

---

[91]Dorsett, *Bounds: Man of Prayer*, 62.

writer. For forty-six years Bounds pastored churches in Tennessee, Alabama, and Missouri. He spent three to four hours each day in prayer.

In 1902 Marshall Brothers in England published his first book *Preacher and Prayer*. He lived to see a second book printed, which was entitled *The Resurrection*. He felt called to a special writing ministry. He spent the last seventeen years of his life reading, writing, and rising before dawn every morning to pray. He prepared books on prayer as well as on Satan and heaven. In 1905 Bounds met Homer W. Hodge who undertook the task of publishing nine more books by Bounds after his death.

Here is a bibliography of the books by Bounds:

1902. *Preacher and Prayer*. This was revised and printed by the Publishing House of the Methodist Episcopal Church, South in 1907 as *Power Through Prayer*.
1907. *The Resurrection*. Reprinted by Schmul Publishers, 2006.
1920. *Purpose in Prayer*.
1921. *Heaven: A Place — A City — A Home*.
1921. *Prayer and Praying Men*.
1922. *Satan: His Personality, Power and Overthrow*. Reprinted by Schmul Publishers, 2015.
1923. *The Possibilities of Prayer*.
1924. *The Reality of Prayer*.
1925. *The Essentials of Prayer*.
1929. *The Necessity of Prayer*.
1931. *Weapons of Prayer*.

In 2004 Baker Books published *The Complete Works of E. M. Bounds on Prayer*, which contains all eight of his books on prayer.

Wesleyan-Arminian Commentaries

Jacob Arminius (1559-1609) was a sixteenth century theologian who reacted against the extremes of Calvinistic theology, especially that the eternal destiny of every person is predestined by God. In contrast to Calvinism, he taught a conditional election — that God chooses all whom he foreknows will trust in him for that salvation, a universal atonement — that Jesus made provision for every person to be saved, preliminary grace — that the Holy Spirit will lead every person to salvation unless they resist him, and conditional perseverance — that we are only saved so long as we continue to trust and obey. The standard exposition of his theology is *Jacob Arminius: Theologian of Grace* by Stanglin and McCall (2012).

In *The Transforming Power of Grace*, Thomas Oden demonstrates that it was the prevailing interpretation of Scripture in the early centuries of the church — with the exception of the later Augustine.[92]

The early followers of Arminius were the Remonstrants. They wrote in Dutch and Latin. Among the Puritans, John Goodwin (1594-1665) was an Arminian but he did not write any commentaries.[93] We really don't have biblical commentaries from an Arminian perspective until the period of classic Methodism.

However, not all Methodists were Arminian. George Whitefield, Griffith Jones, Lady Huntingdon, Daniel Rowland, Howell Harris, and William Williams, for ex-

---

[92]Oden, *Transforming Power*, 152.

[93]However, see his *Christian Theology*, edited by Samuel Dunn (1836).

ample were Calvinistic Methodists.[94] They tended to emphasize evangelism, experience, assurance, and revival more than academic Calvinism. All Wesleyan Methodists are Arminian, but not all Arminians are Methodists.

Free Will or General Baptists are also Arminian, but not Wesleyan. Robert Picirilli edited *The Randall House Bible Commentary* on the New Testament in twelve volumes.

The Christian Church is Arminian, but not Wesleyan. They refer to themselves as the Stone-Campbell Restoration Movement. However, they tend to advocate baptismal regeneration. One of their scholars, Jack Cottrell, has written some helpful things on the Calvinistic-Arminian controversy.

In addition to the Methodist commentaries of John Wesley, and Adam Clarke, Richard Watson wrote an exposition of Matthew, Mark, Luke to 13:15, and Romans to 3:25. He did not live to finish it.

Less known is the commentary of Joseph Benson, published between 1810-1815. Milton S. Terry said Benson's comments were "less critical and learned, but more practical" than Clarke's.

Thomas Coke, sent to American by Wesley as the first superintendent in 1784. He was the father of Methodist missions. His letters and journals have been reprinted. He also produced a six-volume commentary between 1801-1803. Coke's commentary was largely plagiarized from William Dodd. While Dodd's commentary was pronounced as the best available commentary in English by Adam Clarke, unfortunately Dodd lived above his

---

[94]Lloyd-Jones, *The Puritans*, 103.

means and engaged in forgery to finance his lifestyle. For this Dodd was hung.

Joseph Sutcliffe also produced a two-volume commentary in 1824. These commentaries do not necessarily reflect the best in contemporary exegesis, which seems to be an attempt to catalog everything that has been written. However, they often do provide key statements concerning foundational Methodist doctrine.

In 1893 William F. Moulton edited *The Methodist Commentary on the New Testament.*

Henry W. Williams published his exposition of Romans in 1869 and Hebrews in 1871. In 1902 William G. Williams also wrote an exposition on Romans. He should not be confused with the Calvinist Methodist William Williams (1817-1900). Nathanael Burwash published his handbook on Romans in 1887.

J. Agar Beet wrote commentaries on Romans - Philemon. Since these letters of Paul were written to believers they do not deal extensively with eternal punishment. Therefore, Beet's commentaries are relatively safe. When Schmul reprinted Beet's commentary on 1-2 Corinthians, S. D. Herron wrote on the back covers,

> But Beet was not infallible. He was not inspired in the sense the Biblical authors were. With all the deep, scholarly insight and exposition of the Word we will not always agree with him. Neither the publisher nor this writer endorses Beet's interpretation at every point.

George G. Findlay (1849-1919) was another Methodist scholar who wrote commentaries on Galatians, Ephesians, Thessalonians, and the Epistles of John. He was the professor of New Testament Language and Literature at the Wesleyan College in Headingley, West Yorkshire, England.

Thomas O. Summers wrote six volumes covering Matthew - Romans from 1870-1881. William Nast (1807-1899) was a German Methodist who wrote commentaries on Matthew and Mark.

Among American Methodists, Daniel D. Whedon wrote a five-volume commentary on the New Testament which has been reprinted. Whedon edited the *Methodist Quarterly Review* for over twenty years. He also served as general editor for the nine-volume Old Testament commentary. Milton S. Terry wrote three of the volumes; more than any of the other eleven scholars.

R. E. Carroll wrote in 1979,

> Without questioning their devotion to the Lord or their desire and great ability to rightly divide the Word, we still recognize that those twelve able scholars were perhaps over-impressed and over-influenced by the writings of the higher critics.[95]

Schmul quit the project after printing only three of the nine Old Testament volumes (the Pentateuch in two volumes and Psalms). However, Terry's introduction to the Pentateuch was in one of the volumes reprinted. It is a 43-page discussion of higher critical theories which conceded too much to the liberalism of that day.

Amos Binney worked eighteen years to produce *The*

---

[95]Disclaimer found on the back dust jacket of the Schmul reprint.

People's New Testament (1879). Daniel Steele proofed this project.

Joseph Longking (1806-1902), a respected New York Methodist, wrote commentaries on the Gospels, Galatians, Ephesians, and Hebrews.

WESLEYAN STUDY BIBLES

The Wesley Bible. Albert F. Harper, ed. Thomas Nelson, 1990. New King James Version.

While I am in general agreement with most of the comments within this study Bible, my evaluation will be limited to the classic Wesleyan understanding of salvation. Under the section entitled "Baptism with the Holy Spirit" it is acknowledged that John Wesley did not equate Spirit baptism and entire sanctification.

This same section also asserts that John Fletcher equated the baptism of the Holy Spirit with entire sanctification. The truth is that Fletcher spoke of both the new birth and entire sanctification as accomplished by Spirit baptism. In fact, he taught the baptism with the Holy Spirit is repeated as often as necessary between the new birth and the next life.

The writer in the Wesley Bible acknowledged that not all followers of Wesley have made the equation of Spirit baptism and entire sanctification. However, the section concludes with the statement that "the editors of this volume believe there is scriptural support for the view that has been advanced by the holiness movement." They concluded by quoting the classic A. M. Hills statement adopted by the General Holiness Assembly in 1885:

Entire sanctification is a second definite work of grace wrought by the baptism with the Holy Spirit in the heart of the believer subsequently [sic] to regeneration, received instantaneously by faith, by which the heart is cleansed from all corruption and filled with the perfect love of God.

George Failing asked, "Can any comparable definition be found in Wesley's works?"[96] Failing recognized that this was not Wesley's emphasis.

The Hills' statement does not take into account the Wesleyan emphasis that holiness and purity begin with regeneration, that sanctification is both a crisis and a process, that perfection is not a state but a maintained condition, and that the baptism with the Spirit is initiation into Christianity. Hills' definition assumes the doctrine of eradication and does not take into account the command to continuously be full of the Spirit and the promise of continuous cleansing from all sin.

The section on "Sanctification – Initial and Entire" counsels that all Christians should seek the baptism with the Holy Spirit. However, the Bible never commands a believer to receive the baptism of the Holy Spirit. *The Wesley Bible* at this point is neither biblical nor Wesleyan. Instead it reflects a later American holiness perspective.[97]

An adaptation of it, which omitted three essays in the back, called the *Classic Personal Study Bible* (1995;

---

[96]Failing, "Developments in Holiness Theology After Wesley," 23.

[97]See Reasoner, "How Wesleyan is the Wesley Bible," 1-4.

1997) is also out of print. The essays omitted were "Sanctification — Initial and Entire," "Biographies of Significant Quoted Writers," and "The Thirty Texts of Wesley."

The Reflecting God Study Bible. Wayne McCown, ed. Zondervan, 2000. New International Version.

The Christian Holiness Partnership adapted the *NIV Study Bible.* However, the *NIV Study Bible* had a Calvinistic bias. The task of the CHP was to edit and revise the existing notes to provide a distinctively Wesleyan emphasis. The page format could not be changed, however. The writers were to review what was written to determine if the notes included material inappropriate from a Wesleyan point of view and rewrite it, or if some opportunity to express a Wesleyan point of view had been missed to add it. However, regardless of how many words were added or deleted, each page had to end up with the same number of words as the original *NIV Study Bible.* Zondervan accepted most of what was submitted.

Under such limitations, the notes are not that helpful. While the most misleading notes have been edited, all too often opportunities to expound the Wesleyan emphasis are missed. I also missed the quotations from leading Wesleyan writers which were contained in *The Wesley Bible.*

In addition to the notes, there are fifteen essays inserted. These basic introductions, definitely written at a lay level, deal in everyday language with such themes as how to study the Bible and topics of Wesleyan emphasis.

The essays in the *Reflecting God Study Bible* are probably better than those in *The Wesley Bible*, but the notes themselves are not as good.[98]

The Wesley Study Bible. Abingdon, 2009. New Revised Standard Version. Joel B. Green and William H. Willimon, general editors.

This study Bible incorporates Wesley's *Explanatory Notes* and sermons. In general, it seems to avoid theological controversy and emphasize ethical holiness. It also deals with Wesleyan Core Terms and Life Application Topics. It avoids presenting American holiness theology as Wesleyan, which was the weakness of the first study Bible.

Unfortunately, this new study Bible is unnecessarily liberal. There is no reason to use "Before the Common Era" (BCE) and "Common Era" (CE), instead of "Before Christ" (BC) and "In the Year of our Lord" (AD). The greatest historical even in human history was the advent of Jesus Christ.

We are told at Genesis 1:1-2:3 that this is not a scientific explanation for the universe and that the text makes no claim to answer the "how" of creation. Actually, this section does tell us
that God created everything in six days and Hebrews 11:3 tells
us that God created from nothing pre-existent (*ex nihilo*). The problem is that it is just not theologically correct to believe the Bible in the fact of accepted evolutionary theory.

It is unacceptable to claim, as this study Bible does, that the physical love depicted in the Song of Solomon

---

[98]Reasoner, "Reviews," 11-12.

does not describe a married relationship.

Nor is there any reason to divide Isaiah into three parts since it was all written by Isaiah and not piecemeal over several generations in the tradition of Isaiah.

Why cannot this study Bible acknowledge that Peter wrote 2 Peter, when the first verse of the epistle says he did? Why even acknowledge that some scholars do not think Jude wrote the book of Jude which also declares that he did? Why did the editors mar a good project by needlessly capitulating to higher criticism which undermines biblical authority?[99]

SECONDARY LITERATURE

I want to point out the difference between primary and secondary literature. There are many books about John Wesley and they invariably reflect the bias of the author to a greater or lesser extent. Thus, a liberal paints Wesley as a liberal. A charismatic attempts to show Wesley was charismatic. The holiness movement claims Wesley as their founder. Wesley has been presented as basically a Puritan, a Lutheran, a Pelagian, a semi-Pelagian, and a modified Calvinist. There is no substitute for reading Wesley himself.

There is, however, some value in reading a good analysis of Wesley because it gives his background and puts the pieces together showing a bigger picture. There is no rival, for example, to the recently completed four-volume set by Thomas Oden, *John Wesley's Teachings* (2012-2014).

---

[99]Reasoner, "Reviews," 16-17.

Here are a few more such books:

- In 1965 Robert E. Chiles published *Theological Transition in American Methodism* (reprinted in 1983). He traced three major changes in Methodist doctrine from 1790-1935.

  - From Revelation to Reason
  - From Sinful Man to Moral Man
  - From Free Grace to Free Will

Each doctrinal change is traced through three periods of development. Whether the change is viewed as progress or apostasy depends upon our perspective. The first period was that of the founders of Methodism: John Wesley, John Fletcher, Richard Watson, Adam Clarke, and Joseph Benson.

The second period covers the last half of the nineteenth century, culminating in John Miley. By the third period, which brings us up to 1935, Methodism had generally become liberal and had departed from its foundations. Methodism was slower to adopt higher criticism than any other major denomination in Great Britain in the decades prior to World War I. I believe this comparative conservatism may have been due to the heavy emphasis upon Scripture in Methodist liturgy, along with their emphasis on a fervent Christian experience. However, American Methodism was sold out by its educational institutions.

In the section dealing with authority, Chiles establishes Scripture as the basis of early Methodist teaching. However, Wesley certainly allowed for the validity of tradition, reason, and experience to confirm his interpretation of Scripture.

While the authority of Scripture was still affirmed in the next generation of Methodists, there was a growing awe of science and philosophy. By the early twentieth century Methodism has succumb to rationalism based upon evolutionary philosophy.

The early Methodists did not trust reason as their ultimate authority because they believed that human depravity darkened the unregenerate mind. The second major change, however, was in the theology of sin. Early Methodism held to the doctrine of original sin which resulted in total depravity.

By the second period some American Methodist concluded that the doctrine of original sin was too Calvinistic. In this vein, Daniel Whedon wrote *The Freedom of the Will as a Basis of Human Responsibility and a Divine Government* (1864). Thomas Langford wrote that this new stress placed more emphasis upon natural human capability and gave less weight to the orthodox grounding of this ability in prevenient grace.

By the early twentieth century Methodism held that man is a rational being capable of knowing God and entering into fellowship with him apart from his enabling grace. Albert Knudson denied any such thing as an inherited moral depravity. Sin was no longer a necessity. Instead, it was viewed as the mere result of man's free choice. Prevenient grace became understood as the "spark of goodness" within every person. In contrast Chiles concluded that human goodness was Wesley's goal, not his starting point.

This leads to the third major transition — from free grace to free will. If man is depraved, God must make the first move and he does this through preliminary grace.

But if mankind is not sinful, he can choose the true good. Thus, the early Methodist emphasis on prevenient grace was abandoned for an emphasis on free will.

In 1879 John Miley, in at least his own thinking, "fixed" the Methodist doctrine of atonement. He replaced the early Methodist view of satisfaction, with his subjective governmental view which holds that the purpose of the atonement was to impress upon mankind the importance of our right choices.

By the modern period salvation is no longer the rescue of a fallen and helpless humanity. Instead, it was viewed as humanity's free choice to improve their condition. This new doctrine of salvation was not based upon Scripture or tradition, but upon prevailing philosophical liberalism.

- John L. Peters wrote *Christian Perfection and American Methodism* in 1956. It was reprinted by Schmul Publishers. It was originally a doctrinal dissertation at Yale.

At the same time and at the same institution Leland H. Scott wrote "Methodist Theology in America in the Nineteenth Century" (1954). Eldon Dale Dunlap also wrote "Methodist Theology in Great Britain in the Nineteenth Century" in 1956. I have found all three dissertations to be invaluable, in part because the writers seemed to have unlimited access to everything the early Methodists ever wrote. However, only the Peters' book was ever published.

Peters began by attempting to clarify what John Wesley taught concerning Christian perfection. Then he traces the historical record of its proclamation, neglect, modification, or rejection in later Methodism. Albert Outler wrote, "No one has gone much farther than Peters in linking the American Methodists with Wesley and his sources."

• While Peters is primarily historical, Harald Lindström, *Wesley and Sanctification* is primarily doctrinal. Lindström completed his dissertation in Swedish in 1946, attracting attention in *The Journal of Religion* as early as 1948. He was a student of Anders Nygren. He was the first Methodist to be appointed to a theological faculty in any Swedish university, serving as professor of dogmatic theology at Uppsala University. His book, *Wesley and Sanctification*, was first published in English in 1956. Francis Asbury Press reprinted it in 1980.

In addition to the research of Thomas Albin, Kevin Watson has written on the class meeting system of early Methodism. See also Lester Ruth on Methodist worship.

Solomon declared, "Of making many books there is no end, and much study is a weariness of the flesh" (Eccl 12:12). Yet Wesley admonished his lay preachers contract a taste for reading by use, or return to their trade.[100]

---

[100]Wesley, *BE Works*, 10:340. Annual Minutes, 1766.

GLOSSARY OF TERMS

AFFUSION — the method of baptism where water is poured on the head of the person being baptized. The word *affusion* comes from the Latin *affusio*, meaning *to pour on*. Thus, it symbolizes the outpouring of the Holy Spirit as described in Romans 5:5.

ANTIMONIANISM. *Nomos* is the Greek word for *law*. The prefix *anti* means *against*. To be *against the law* is to teach that under the gospel dispensation the moral law is of no use or obligation because faith alone is necessary to salvation. We are initially saved by faith alone, but God's saving grace will enable us to keep his commandments (see 1 John 2:3-6). John Fletcher wrote *Checks to Antinomianism* in the eighteenth century. Although the term *antinomian* is not used as much today, the doctrine is still preached.

APOSTASY. This word describes a departure from the faith. It is impossible for a person to depart from a faith they never possessed. Yet this concept clashes with the doctrine of the unconditional security of the believer. Therefore, there are several theological attempts to explain the scriptural warning against apostasy.

ARMINIAN. Jacob or James Arminius was a sixteenth century theologian who reacted against the extremes of Calvinistic theology, especially that the eternal destiny of every person is predestined by God. In contrast to Calvinism, he taught a conditional election, a universal atonement, preliminary grace, and conditional perseverance. John Wesley was Arminian in theology and named his magazine *The Arminian Magazine.*

AUGUSTINE. A theologian of the fourth and fifth centuries who debated with Pelagius on the issue of free will. Augustine denied freedom of the will, teaching that God predestined those who would be saved. Martin Luther and John Calvin were influenced by the philosophy of Augustine.

THE AWAKENED STATE. The preliminary ministry of the Holy Spirit convicts the sinner of his sin, his lack of righteousness, and the impending judgment. No longer asleep to his true spiritual state, the awakened sinner can do nothing to save himself but is enabled through divine grace to repent and believe. To a greater or lesser degree every soul is enlightened or awakened at some point in their life. The harder he tries to reform himself the more he will become conscious of his bondage to sin.

CALVINISM. Based on the theology of John Calvin, a sixteenth century reformer. Calvin taught a logical chain of doctrines beginning with **total depravity** — the doctrine that Adam's original act of sin so affected the human race that mankind is born with a bias toward sin. Sin has so permeated our total personality that there is nothing in man that has not been infected by the power of sin. Wesleyans do not disagree with Calvinists at this point. However, Calvin also taught **unconditional election**—the doctrine that God has predestined those he will save. **Limited atonement** asserts that Christ only atoned for the sins of those God predestined to be saved. **Irresistible grace** teaches that those God has chosen and for whom Christ died will experience an irresistible call by the Holy

Spirit. It is impossible that these will be lost since God has decreed their salvation. They will **persevere** and will be eternally secure.

CATHOLIC. This word means *universal* and describes the universal church. Protestants affirm that the church is *catholic*. However, the term *Roman Catholic* refers to a denomination with headquarters in Rome.

CHARISMATIC. The Greek word for gift, *charisma*, describes the gifts of the Holy Spirit. The modern charismatic movement began in 1960 with an emphasis on one gift — the gift of tongues, which was introduced into mainline denominations. While cessationists believe that the extraordinary gifts of the Spirit died out after the early church era, the modern charismatic movement tended to over-emphasize the extra-ordinary gifts. Wesley put more emphasis on the fruit of the Spirit, but was not a cessationist. Rob Staples explained that Wesleyans believe in the gifts of the Spirit. "Thus we, too, are charismatics. But we are charismatics *who do not speak in unknown tongues*."[101]

CESSATIONISM. The belief that miracles ceased after the early church era. This position is held by many, but not all, Calvinists.

CHRISTIAN PERFECTION. While absolute perfection is an attribute of God alone, Christ commands his disciples to be perfect (Matt 5:48). This perfection is a relative perfection, a perfection imputed to believers when they

---

[101] Staples, "Rose is a Rose," 25.

love God completely and love their neighbor as themselves. This is *Christian* perfection.

COMPATIBILISTIC FREEDOM OF THE WILL. The Calvinist position that man's freedom is compatible with God's determinism. Thus, while man is free to act according to his own choices, since he is totally depraved he will always choose to sin. Sin is therefore his only choice.

CONNECTIONAL. The autonomy of the local congregation must be balanced by the concept of inter-dependence and connection. Connectionalism implies a level of the church beyond the local congregation. Thus, the church is not simply a voluntary association of like-minded individuals; as the body of Christ there is a connection. Methodism has always been a connectional system. The British spelling, however, is *connexional*. Those churches and ministers within the connexion meet in annual conference. Thus, conference, circuits, and class meetings all promoted fellowship beyond the local church within early Methodism.

DEISM teaches that God is transcendent and does not intervene in human affairs. Thus, they would deny the concept of particular or meticulous providence. Deism rejects the possibility of miracles. This view was popular in the eighteenth century. It fits with the modern concept of theistic evolution.

DISPENSATIONALISM is a recent type of premillennialism which emphasizes a distinction between Israel and the church based upon the belief that covenants are unconditional. They believe that God in history had multiple plans of salvation, which are called dispensations. Dispensational scholars do not agree among themselves as to how many dispensations there are, but these "dispensations" are defined as a span of time marked by a different method of divine dealing with man. Since the Jews reject Christ's kingdom, dispensationalists believe that it was postponed. The church dispensation is a parenthesis in God's plan. Therefore, the church must be raptured out of this world before Christ will return and set up his kingdom with the Jews.

For dispensationalists, the kingdom is future and contingent upon the return of Christ. This interpretation began with John Darby in 1830 and was popularized in America by the *Scofield Reference Bible*. According to Scofield, "a dispensation is a period of time during which man is tested in respect to his obedience to some specific revelation of the will of God." They see these dispensations as all ending in failure.

ECUMENICAL. This term originated from the Greek word *oikoumene* which meant "the whole inhabited world." There were seven ecumenical general church councils in early church history: two at Nicaea, three at Constantinople, one each at Ephesus and Chalcedon. In the twentieth century the modern ecumenical movement was an attempt to promote church unity among denominations. Some wanted to bring all churches under one organization and this goal of unity was often at the expense of orthodox doctrine. This concern caused fundamentalists to react to the World Council of Churches, formed in 1948.

EFFECTUAL CALLING. The call to salvation is as universal as the atonement. Those who advocate limited atonement must make an artificial distinction between the general call, the proclamation of the free offer of grace, and the effectual call, which regenerates only the elect. There is no good news for the reprobate, and to proclaim the gospel to them is actually disingenuous for Calvinism.

ENTHUSIAST. Originally the term meant to be inspired by God (*en* + *theos*). In Wesley's day it had come to mean religious fanaticism. Today enthusiasm does not have a negative connotation, but instead is used to refer to zeal or excitement. The term *fanatic* in Latin also meant *inspired by a deity*. However, today it means excessive enthusiasm and intense, uncritical devotion.

EPISCOPAL. Based on the Greek word *episkopos*, which means overseer or bishop, an episcopal form of government implies a level of leadership above the local pastor.

ESCHATOLOGY is based on the Greek word *eschatos*, which means *last things*. Eschatology includes such fundamental doctrines as the second coming of Christ, the resurrection and judgment, heaven and hell. Eschatology is God's plan for the establishment and victory of his church.

EXISTENTIALISM. A philosophy dealing with existence and emphasizing experience. Søren Kierkegaard, a Danish philosopher writing in the nineteenth century, is often considered the father of existentialism. Human experience is beyond science and philosophy, but it is experience which gives meaning within a meaningless world. While Methodist theology emphasizes Christian experience, that experience must be understood in the framework of biblical revelation.

EX NIHILO. This Latin phrase describes creation from nothing. Either God or matter must be eternal. Christianity teaches that God is eternal and spoke the cosmos into existence through divine decree.

FILIOQUE. This Latin word means *and the Son*. It describes a double procession of the Holy Spirit from the Father *and the Son*. This became controversial when the Western church added this phrase to the Nicene Creed. Yet John 15:26 seems to teach this double procession.

FIVE *SOLAS* of the REFORMATION.

* *Sola scriptura* means that the Bible is our highest authority — not tradition, reason, or experience. While the Bible is not the only source of truth, it is the test of all truth. Those who deny the principle of *sola scriptura* are not truly Protestant.
* *Sola fide* means that we are saved through faith alone in Jesus Christ. This is affirmed in Romans 3:21-28.
* *Sola gratia* means that we are saved by the grace of God alone. We can do nothing to merit salvation.
* *Sola Christus* means that Jesus Christ alone is our Lord, Savior, and King.
* *Sola Dei Gloria* means that we live for the glory of God alone.

FUNDAMENTALISM is the concept that there is an irreducible minimum statement of Christian doctrine and that these doctrines should be defended. The great ecumenical creeds of the Christian church set forth fundamental Christian doctrine. Wesley spoke of some of these doctrines as "those grand, fundamental doctrines, original sin, justification by faith, the new birth, inward and outward holiness." While we affirm personal Christian experience, we also affirm the historic Christian creeds which state the Christian faith objectively.

Essentially the Puritans were the fundamentalists of the seventeenth century and the Methodists were the fundamentalists of the eighteenth century.

In the nineteenth century there was an attempt by liberals to reinterpret Christian doctrine so as to reconcile it with evolutionary theory. In reaction to this trend a set of books was published in 1910-1915 called *The Fundamentals*. This set of books was a collection of ninety articles written by a broad coalition of scholars who defended the existence of God, the inspiration and inerrancy of Scripture, the deity of Christ, his incarnation and virgin birth, his dual nature, the historical reality of his miracles, his bodily resurrection, the personality and deity of the Holy Spirit, sin, substitutionary atonement, grace, justification by faith, regeneration, discipleship, consecration, the church, Satan, prayer, evangelism, preaching, and missions.

Eventually this twentieth-century movement was identified with a more sectarian viewpoint. It became known sometimes for its harsh criticisms and separatist mentality. In some circles *fundamentalism* became associated with a rejection of all translations except the King James Version, an inclusion of the doctrine of eternal security as a fundamental doctrine, or advocating dispensationalism.

The inherent danger within fundamentalism is that it becomes merely reactionary and that it unites on the basis of what it opposes. Regardless of the label, we dare not abandon the fundamentals of the faith — call them what you will — basic, core, cardinal, essential, rudimentary, foundational, orthodox, or fundamental.

IMPARTED RIGHTEOUSNESS. The infusion of a new nature when we are born again is the positive side of salvation. Forgiveness is the non-imputation of our sins to our account. Both come together. God does not impute to us what he does not also impart to us.

IMPUTED RIGHTEOUSNESS. When we trust in the atoning work of Christ, God no longer imputes our sins to our account. Thus, we are forgiven. However, the Bible does not teach that God imputes the righteousness of Christ to our accounts in lieu of any personal holiness.

INERRANCY. The Bible itself claims to be inspired, infallible, and absolutely pure. Its truth is confirmed by the testimony of the Holy Spirit. Its contents are historically reliable and internally consistent. Its revelation corresponds to human experience. Its teachings are confirmed by miracles, authenticated by fulfilled prophecy, and accepted by Jesus Christ.

The Word of God is trustworthy because God cannot err. The ministry of the Holy Spirit in the process of inspiration was to ensure that the human authors accurately recorded God's revelation. The purpose of divine inspiration was to insure that the human authors accurately recorded God's words.

INSPIRATION. According to 2 Timothy 3:16, all Scripture is inspired. The Greek word θεόπνευστος (*theopneustos*) means God-breathed. This process of inspiration describes the supernatural influence of the Holy Spirit, ensuring that the human author was restrained from error and guided to write the words of God. According to 2 Peter 1:21 the human authors were carried along by the Holy Spirit. This is the most complete description of divine inspiration. Yet there is a mystery about this process. It was apparently not mechanical or uniform. The Holy Spirit did not override human personality. The vocabulary and style of the human authors varies. Some portions of Scripture were given by dictation. Some sections were eyewitness accounts. Parts of Scripture were based on oral tradition, previous documentation, or ordinary sources of information such as government documents or even a census. Solomon and Luke both did research. In other instances, the prophets probably did not fully understand the message they were given. Yet every part and genre of Scripture was fully inspired by God. While inspiration involved a divine/human interaction, it is clear that God is in control of the process which was superintended by the Holy Spirit.

While the terms *revelation* and *inspiration* are sometimes used interchangeably, *inspiration* denotes the agency of the Holy Spirit. The Son reveals the Father; the Spirit inspires the Word of God to be written by the prophets and apostles. The function of the Holy Spirit was to ensure that the words which were written accurately represented God's intention.

The purpose of inspiration was to ensure accuracy and avoid error. To claim that the Holy Scriptures are not trustworthy impugns the work of the Holy Spirit. It also sets up human authorities above the final authority of Scripture itself. The Bible is infallible because it is the Word of God. There must be one ultimate authority by which all other truth claims are evaluated. The Scriptures are the final authority by which tradition, experience, and reason are tested.

JUSTIFICATION. This word describes the forgiveness of sin which occurs when we trust in Christ alone. Our sins are no longer imputed against us through the merits of Christ's atonement.

KINGDOM of GOD *or* **KINGDOM of HEAVEN** refers to the rule of God over his people. A kingdom is the realm, and the people of the realm, over which a king exercises authority. The kingdom of God exists wherever the will of God is done. We enter the kingdom of God through the new birth (John 3:5). This kingdom expands as more people are born again. Thus, it is both a present reality and a future hope.

LAPSARIAN VIEWS. Calvinism has speculated on the chronological order of God's decrees regarding election. *Supralapsarianism* holds that *before* creation God foreordained certain individuals to everlasting life and others to eternal destruction. Unless eternal perdition is somehow defined as good, the supralapsarian position holds that God decreed something for evil. Thus, reprobation precedes sin.

Infralapsarianism teaches that *after* creation, God decreed the salvation of the elect. Therefore, the main difference is whether the decree to save the elect comes before or after the fall. Arminius concluded that infralapsarianism also fails to avoid the conclusion that God is the author of sin.[102] He asked, "Does the Justice of God permit Him to destine to death eternal a rational creature, who has never sinned? We reply in the negative."[103]

The Bible does not address the issue of an order of God's decrees. This is nothing more than speculative theology.

LATITUDINARIANISM. A seventeenth century movement which tried to find a middle ground between Anglicans, Presbyterians, and Dissenters in England. They tended to sacrifice doctrinal purity in order to promote cooperation. Over time the second generation enlightenment leaders abandoned Christianity for relativism or rationalism. They advocated "speculative latitudinarianism" which advocated that people should think and let think. Perhaps the twentieth century ecumenical movement would be open to some of the same criticism.

LEGALISM is an attempt to earn salvation through works or to make oneself holy through extra-biblical rules and standards.

LIBERALISM or *modernism* refers to the worldview which began with the French Enlightenment period and ended with the fall of communism. Liberalism demanded a closed system in which all phenomena had to be explained within the parameters of natural causes. Thus, it

---

[102]Arminius, *Works*, 1:648.

[103]Arminius, *Works*, 2:352.

rejected the possibility of miracles. Liberalism emphasized reason and experience over Scripture and tradition.

LIBERTARIAN FREEDOM OF THE WILL. In contrast
to compatibilistic freedom, this position states that God
confers upon us the freedom of contrary choice. Thus, our
actions are foreknown, but not predestined by God. This
is the Arminian position.

LITURGY. The form which is followed in public worship. Those who claim not to be liturgical tend to follow
the same rut, even though it is not planned or written.

MEANS of GRACE. The divinely ordained channels
through which God's grace is received. Wesley distinguished between the instituted means of grace which are
works of piety ordained by God and the prudential means
of grace which are spontaneous, practical works of mercy.

MILLENNIUM. This term is based on the Latin word for
thousand. The Greek word used in Revelation 20:1-6 to
refer to a period of a thousand years is *chilia.* The Latin
term for a thousand-year period is *millennium.* Differing
interpretations of this passage have produced differing
millennial views. Historically the terms *millenarians,*
chiliasts, and *adventists* have all referred to premillennialists.

Premillennialists teach that this millennial period of
time begins with the return of Christ. Postmillennialists
believe Christ returns *after* this period of time.
Amillennialists believe this period of time marks the time
between Christ's first and second coming. All postmillennialists are amillennial in the sense that they deny the

literal physical reign of Christ on earth. And all amillennialists are postmillennial with regard to the timing of Christ's return.

Both amillennialists and postmillennialists understand this as an indefinite period of time which refers to the spiritual reign of Christ from heaven. Premillennialists understand this as a definite period of time when Christ reigns from a throne in Jerusalem.

MONERGISM means that only one person is working, in contrast to *synergism*. Calvinism teaches that since man is unable to do anything to save himself, God must first regenerate him and then he will repent and believe *after* he is born again. A proper understanding of preliminary grace renders monergism an unnecessary position logically. However, it is still true that God must initiate the salvation process.

MORAVIAN. The Moravian movement traces its roots back to John Huss. The reformation begun by Huss was continued by the formation of "The Brethren" in 1457. After being almost wiped out by the Counter Reformation, in 1722 Count Nicholas Ludwig Zinzendorf invited the Brethren in Moravia and Bohemia to escape persecution and emigrate to land he owned in Germany. They built a town called Herrnhut and from this base sent missionaries all over the world. Wesley met a group of Moravians on his return home from Georgia, and prior to his Aldersgate conversion he was discipled by Peter Böhler, a Moravian.

MYSTICISM is an emphasis on subjective personal experience rather than the objective Word of God. Wesley said, "I think the rock on which I had the nearest made shipwreck of the faith was the writings of the Mystics."[104] Yet he also emphasized the importance of a personal relationship with God. For some the witness of the Spirit or the leading of the Spirit is mysticism. Mysticism becomes dangerous when it leads people to arrive at doctrinal conclusions which are based on their own revelation and which contradict the revelation of the Scriptures.

ORDO SALUTIS. The order of salvation. According to Calvinism, predestination and election are followed by effectual calling. The first subjective step is then regeneration, followed by repentance and faith.

The Wesleyan-Arminian *order salutis* is quite different. Through the preliminary grace of God we are awakened, convicted, and called. This work of the Holy Spirit also enables us to repent and believe.

When we respond to the divine initiative, God brings forth new life. Then we are justified, regenerated, adopted, and assured of our salvation. The Holy Spirit continues to lead us to a deeper work of sanctification and Christian perfection.

ORIGINAL GUILT. While we share the effects of the fall, this phrase deals with whether the human race incurs the guilt of Adam's fall. Arminius rejected original guilt. Wesley taught that original guilt was cancelled as an unconditional benefit of the atonement.

ORIGINAL SIN. This term describes the corrupt nature that mankind inherited due to Adam's original act of sin.

---

[104]Wesley, *Letter* to Samuel Wesley, 23 Nov 1736.

Pelagianism and liberalism reject this doctrine, affirming instead the basic goodness of mankind.

PATRISTICS is the study of the writings of the church fathers of the first five centuries, especially Athanasius, Basil, Gregory of Nazianzen, John Chrysostom, Ambrose, Augustine, Jerome and Gregory the Great — the eight doctors of the early church.

PELAGIAN. Pelagius was a late fourth century theologian who taught that Adam was created spiritually neutral and that Adam's sin injured only himself. Each person enters the world without inherited depravity and can choose either good or evil. Salvation is based upon human choice and not divine grace. Man has the ability to fulfill all that God requires. Augustine challenged Pelagius, and perhaps the humanism of Pelagius caused Augustine to overreact, moving to a fatalistic position of predestination. Pelagianism was formally condemned as a heresy by the General Council of Ephesus in AD 431.

PENAL. The word refers to the punishment for breaking the law. It is employed in the doctrine of the atonement to describe the necessity for satisfaction of the law of God. Penal substitution means that Christ was punished for our sins. Some theologians object to an over-emphasis on forensic language. However, there is a legal aspect in salvation which corresponds to justification.

PLENARY INSPIRATION. The term *plenary* means that Scripture is fully inspired — not simply the sections which speak to us.

POSTMODERNISM. The final attempt to implement modernism went down with the collapse of communism. Science and technology failed to save us. The postmodern world is more open to the supernatural, but it has rejected Christianity, instead importing eastern mysticism and new age teaching.

Postmodernism is relativistic. Everyone has his own story, his own reality. Ultimate reality is unknowable, only your perspective. If everyone has his own reality, the result is a world of isolation. For many people reality is cyberspace. Since we all have a different frame of reference, we can never completely understand each other.

For postmodernism, every perspective is equally valid. There is no author and no ideals. There is no grand story. There is no hope. Thus, the only absolute is that there are no transcendent absolutes — only situational ethics. Emotions rule over reason; and regardless of what the Bible says, we should go with our feelings and not with propositional truth.

Even the Bible is interpreted with a hermeneutic of suspicion. This means that while the apostle Paul gave his opinion of right and wrong, we must also strive to understand the point of view of his opponents. Who is to say that Jewish society was better than that of the surrounding nations? The Bible only gives one viewpoint. What is good for the conquering nation may be bad for the defeated nation. Old Testament history was written by conquering Israel.

Postmodernism is pluralistic. We believe everyone should have the freedom to practice the religion of their choice, even if their religion is a belief in nothing besides themselves.

The postmodern worldview is relational. To "be" is to be in relation. Personhood is largely determined and shaped in terms of relationships. While relational theology may be helpful, it has led to an "openness" to process theology. The result is that God is so much a part of the world that he is no longer transcendent from his creation. He will become all in all only when the world's redemption is complete. In the mean time sin causes an alienation within him because he is so identified with his fallen creation.

PREVENIENT is from two Latin words, *prae*—before and *venire*—to come. Preventing or prevenient grace, as used by Wesley, means the grace of God which precedes or comes before human action. The grace of God precedes the human response of faith. Based on the doctrine of total depravity, Calvinism concluded that God must first save the elect before they could repent and believe. Wesley understood that the grace of God enables a sinner to repent and believe. In more modern language the equivalent term would be *preliminary.*

PROTESTANT. John Wycliffe first coined this term with his book *Protestatio* in 1378 in protest of abuses within Roman Catholicism. The Protestant Reformation spanned the fourteenth to seventeenth centuries. While October 31, 1517, the day Martin Luther posted his Ninety-Five Theses, is often considered the birth of the Reformation, Wycliffe is properly called "the morning star of the Reformation." The English Reformation was blunted by the politics of the Anglican Church and did not reach its fruition until the eighteenth century Methodist revival. Reformation theology is summarized in the five *solas.*

QUADRILATERAL. Properly understood, this term describes the primacy of scriptural authority, complemented by tradition, reason, and experience. The term was coined by Albert Outler in 1964 and has since often been distorted to imply that there are four equal sources of authority. Liberalism has tended to shop for the source that they think best supports their opinions.

REGENERATION. The impartation of spiritual life results in the new birth. We are raised from spiritual death to spiritual life through the infusion of the Holy Spirit.

REVELATION. Our knowledge of God is based on his self-disclosure. While philosophy is mankind's attempt to discover truth, *revelation* means that God took the initiative to make himself known. His revelation initially took the form of direct communication, then his revelation through Jesus Christ, and finally the inspiration of the Holy Spirit.

SACERDOTAL. The belief that salvation comes through the sacraments administered by the church. Only priests authorized by their church may administer the sacraments and thus they hold a monopoly on salvation. Such views contradict the catholicity of the church, the role of Christ as our high priest, and the priesthood of all believers.

SACRAMENTS. A sacrament is a symbolic ritual which was instituted by Christ and is commanded for his church to observe. Both baptism and the Lord's Supper meet the criteria of a sacrament. They serve as signs and seals of the covenant and are a means of grace. They are more than ordinances, but they are less than salvific.

SACRAMENTALISM exalts the sacraments to the point that faith for salvation is placed in the proper observance of ritual. While the sacraments are a means of grace, participating in baptism or the Lord's Supper does not automatically result in conversion.

SANCTIFICATION The Hebrew word *qadosh* describes the state of consecration that existed when a person or object was set apart or separated for holy use. In the New Testament *hagiasmos* does not refer primarily to a ritual act, but to a moral condition. When the word *sanctification* is found in Scripture it usually refers to initial sanctification unless qualified by another word such as *entire* or *wholly*. *Initial sanctification* is closely related to regeneration. When a person truly believes, he or she is justified, regenerated, and initially sanctified.

Progressive sanctification refers to the gradual process in which the Holy Spirit reveals to a Christian his or her sinful nature and their deeper need of God's grace. Through this process there is a growth in Christlikeness and a gradual cleansing which produces holy character.

Entire sanctification is the condition of loving God with all your heart. This love expels all sin, cleansing the heart from all unrighteousness. Wesley felt that this was the privilege of all Christians and that all should strive for it. A person in this condition has attained Christian perfection. However, neither entire sanctification nor Christian perfection imply the end of growth or progress.

Final sanctification denotes an absolute perfection which will occur after the resurrection when we are raised with glorified bodies, no longer under the curse, subject to temptation or infirmities and delivered from the very presence of sin.

SCRIPTURE or **SCRIPTURES**. The term *Scripture* refers to the body of sixty-six books which were inspired by the Holy Spirt and contain God's revelation to mankind. When used in the plural, S*criptures* refer to the sixty-six books.

SEMI-PELAGIAN. This position accepts the doctrine of original sin, but believes that mankind inherently has the power to repent and believe without preliminary grace.

SEMI-AUGUSTINIAN. This position holds that man has no ability to save himself. Therefore, God must initiate the process and man can be saved only when the Holy Spirit provides saving faith. However, unlike the full Augustinian position which is also Calvinism, this position rejects monergism. This is the true Wesleyan-Arminian position, which Augustine also held before his debates with Pelagius.

SINFUL NATURE. The tendency toward sin which we inherited from Adam. This amounts to a depravity which affects every facet of our personhood and renders us completely unable to save ourselves. However, it should not be understood as a substance which can be eradicated. The Bible does not refer to "carnality" as an entity. Rather, this sinful nature is a twist, a distortion, and inward bent that puts our will above God's will.

SOLIFIDIANISM. The sixteenth century reformers taught *sola fide* (faith alone) was necessary for salvation. Since man is dead in sin, even faith is the gift of God. While Wesleyanism believes we are initially justified by faith alone, it also teaches we are finally justified by works. The danger of an overemphasis on faith can lead to a mere intellectual assent which produces no conversion or a one-time decision which produces no fruit. John Fletcher warned that a solifidian maintains we are completely and eternally saved by faith alone "in so unscriptural a manner as to make good works unnecessary to eternal salvation; representing the law of Christ as a mere rule of life; and calling all those who consider that law as a rule of judgment, legalists, Pharisees, or heretics." Fletcher cautioned that it is a softer word for antinomianism. Even Melanchthon, the Lutheran theologian, declared that we are justified by faith alone, but that faith is not alone (*Sola fides justificat, sed fides non est sola*).

SOTERIOLOGY. The Greek word for salvation is σωτηρία (*soteria*). Thus, the doctrines of salvation are referred to as soteriology.

SUPEREROGATION A Roman Catholic teaching that Christ exceeded what was necessary for man's salvation. Additionally, the saints also suffered beyond what was required of them for their salvation. The surplus goes into a treasury of merit which is under the control of the Roman Catholic church. At the discretion of the Pope, those who fall short of good works may draw upon this treasury. The system of selling indulgences was based upon this dogma.

SYNERGISM. This concept means that man is enabled to respond and work with the Holy Spirit due to preliminary grace. Therefore, although we are dead in sin we are enabled to cooperate, fulfilling the demands to repent and believe, as we are empowered by the Holy Spirit.

TOTAL DEPRAVITY. As the result of man's original sin through Adam, we inherit a sinful nature which renders us completely unable to save ourselves. Our depravity is total since it affects our entire being — our intellect, our emotions, and our will.

TULIP acrostic. The doctrines of Calvinism are often enumerated through the use of the TULIP acrostic.
   T - total depravity
   U - unconditional election
   L -limited or particular atonement
   I - irresistible grace
   P - perseverance of the saints.

Calvinism sees this as an unbroken logical chain. However, only the first point is taught in Scripture.

WITNESS of the SPIRIT. The direct assurance of the Holy Spirit to the believer that he is forgiven and accepted by God. This direct assurance is corroborated by the indirect witness of a good conscience.

BIBLIOGRAPHY

Abbey, C. J. and J. H. Overton. *The English Church in the Eighteenth Century.* 2 vols. London: Longmans, Green, 1878.

Albin, Thomas R. "An Empirical Study of Early Methodist Spirituality." *Wesleyan Theology Today.* Theodore Runyon, ed. Nashville: Kingswood, 1985.

Asbury, Francis. *The Causes, Evils, and Cures of Heart and Church Divisions.* Philadelphia: Parry Hall, 1792. Reprint, Nicholasville, KY: Schmul, 2022.

_____. *The Journal and Letters of Francis Asbury.* 3 vols. Elmer T. Clark, ed. Nashville: Abingdon, 1958.

Bangs, Nathan. *The Necessity, Nature, and Fruits of Sanctification in a Series of Letters to a Friend.* 1851. Reprint, Salem, OH: Allegheny, 2006.

Banks, John S. *A Manual of Christian Doctrine.* London: Charles H. Kelly, 1902.

Beet, Joseph Agar. *A Manual of Theology.* London: Hodder and Stoughton, 1906.

_____. *A Commentary on St. Paul's Epistle to the Romans.* 10th ed. 1902. Reprint, Salem, OH: Allegheny, 1982. Between 1877 and 1902 there were ten editions of Beet's *Commentary* on Romans.

_____. *A Commentary on St. Paul's Epistles to the Corinthians*. 1882. Reprinted in two volumes, Salem, OH: Schmul, 1988-1989.

_____. *A Commentary on St. Paul's Epistle to the Galatians*. 1903. Reprint, Salem, OH; Schmul, 1976.

_____. *A Commentary on St. Paul's Epistles to the Ephesians, Philippians, Colossians, and to Philemon*. 1890. Reprint, Salem, OH: Schmul, n. d.

Benson, Joseph. *Sermons, and Plans of Sermons, of Many of the Most Important Texts of Holy Scripture*. Jabez Bunting, ed. 7 vols. Baltimore: Armstrong & Plaskitt, 1827.

_____. *The Life of John Fletcher*. 2nd ed. Reprint, Salem, OH: Allegheny, 1984.

Binney, Amos. *Binney's Theological Compend Improved*. Nashville: Abingdon, 1875.

_____ and Daniel Steele. *The People's Commentary on the New Testament*. New York: Eaton & Mains, 1878.

Brush, Robert L. and Vic Reasoner, eds. *The Wesley Workbook*. 1996. Reprint, Evansville, IN: Fundamental Wesleyan, 2025.

Burtner, Robert W. and Robert E. Chiles. *A Compend of Wesley's Theology*. New York: Abingdon, 1954.

Burwash, Nathanael, ed. Wesley's Doctrinal Standards. Toronto:
William Briggs, 1881. Reprint, *Wesley's 52 Standard Sermons*. Salem, OH: Schmul, 1967.

_____. *Manual of Christian Theology on the Inductive Method*. 2 vols. London: Horace Marshall & Son, 1900

Carpenter, William, ed. Introduction by George Marsden. *Wesleyana: A Complete System of Wesleyan Theol-*

ogy; Selected from the Writings of the Rev. John Wesley, A.M. and so Arranged as to Form a Miniature Body of Divinity. Revised, Enlarged, and an Index Added. New York: T. Mason and G. Lane, 1825. Reprint, Salem, OH: Allegheny Wesleyan Methodist Connection, 1979.

Carter, David. "Joseph Agar Beet and the Eschatological Crisis." *Proceedings of the Wesleyan Historical Society* 51:6 (October 1998) 197-216.

Cartwright, Peter. *Autobiography of Peter Cartwright.* 1856. Reprint, Nashville: Abingdon, 1984.

Carvosso, William. *The Efficacy of Faith in the Atonement of Christ: Exemplified in A Memoir of Mr. William Carvosso, Sixty Years a Class-Leader in the Wesleyan Methodist Connexion.* 1836. Reprint, Shoals, IN: Kingsley, 1996.

Chiles, Robert E. *Theological Transition in American Methodism: 1790-1935.* 1965. Reprint, Lanham, MD: University Press of America, 1983.

Clarke, Adam. *Clavis Biblica.* 1820. Reprint, *The Christian Prophet and His Work.* Salem, OH: Schmul, 1999.

_____. *The Holy Bible, Containing the Old and New Testaments: The Text Carefully Printed from the Most Correct Copies of the Present Authorized Translations, Including the Marginal reading and Parallel Tests; with a Commentary and Critical Notes, Designed as a help to a Better Understanding of the Sacred Writings.* 6 vols. 1811-1825. Reprint, Nashville: Abingdon, 1950.

_____. *The Miscellaneous Works of Adam Clarke.* 13 vols. James Everett, ed. London: Thomas Tegg, 1836-1837.

Coke, Thomas. *The Letters of Dr. Thomas Coke.* John A. Vickers, ed. Nashville: Kingswood, 2013.

_____. *The Journals of Dr. Thomas Coke.* John A. Vickers, ed. Nashville: Kingswood, 2005.

Collins, Kenneth J. *Wesley on Salvation.* Grand Rapids: Francis Asbury, 1989.

_____. *A Real Christian: The Life of John Wesley.* Nashville: Abingdon, 1999.

Cooke, William. *Christian Theology: its Doctrines and Ordinances Explained and Defended.* London: Hamilton, Adams, and Co, 1863.

Coppedge, Allan. *John Wesley in Theological Debate.* Wilmore, KY: Wesley Heritage, 1987.

Cox, Leo. *John Wesley's Concept of Perfection.* Kansas City: Beacon Hill, 1964.

Davies, Rupert E, A. Raymond George, and Gordon Rupp, eds. *A History of the Methodist Church in Great Britain.* 4 vols. London: Epworth, 1998.

Dunlap, Elden Dale. "Methodist Theology in Great Britain." PhD diss, Yale University, 1956.

Dunn, Samuel, ed. *Christian Theology.* 1835. Reprint, Salem, OH: Schmul, 1967.

Etheridge, J. W. *The Life of the Rev. Adam Clarke, LLD.* Nashville: Southern Methodist Publishing House, 1859.

Failing, George E. "Developments in Holiness Theology After Wesley." *Insights Into Holiness.* Kenneth Geiger, ed. 1963. Reprint, Salem, OH: Schmul, 1989.

Field, Benjamin. *The Student's Handbook of Christian Theology.* London: Hodder and Stroughton, 1870. Reprint, Freeport, PA: Fountain, 1957.

Fitzgerald, O. P. *Dr. Summers: A Life-Study.* Nashville: Southern Methodist Publishing House, 1886.

Fletcher, John. *The Works of the Reverend John Fletcher.* 1833. Reprint, Salem, OH: Schmul, 1974.

Foster, Randolph Sinks. *Studies in Theology.* New York: Eaton & Mains, 1889-1899.

_____. *Beyond the Grave.* New York: Phillips & Hunt, 1879.

Gunter, W. Stephen. *Arminius and His* Declaration of Sentiments: *An Annotated Translated with Introduction and Theological Commentary.* Waco, TX: Baylor University Press 2012.

Hannah, John. *Introductory Lectures on the Study of Christian Theology:With Outlines of Lectures on the Doctrines of Christianity.* London: Wesleyan Conference Office, 1872.

Hare, Edward. *Genuine Methodism acquitted and spurious Methodism condemned, in six letters addressed to J. Cooke, in answer to his vindication of his sermons, ironically entitled Methodism Condemned by Methodist preachers.* Rochdale, England: J. Hartley, 1807.

_____. *A Treatise on the Scriptural Doctrine of Justification.* New York: Methodist Episcopal Church. 1841.

_____. *The principal doctrines of Christianity defended against the errors of Socinianism: Being an Answer to the Rev. John Grundy's Lectures.* New York: Methodist Episcopal Church, 1837.

_____. *An apology for continuing in the steadfast belief of the eternal sonship of our Lord and Saviour Jesus Christ : in a letter to the Rev. Joseph Benson.* London: James Nichols, 1818.

_____. *The Scriptural Doctrine of Assurance, as taught by the Methodists*. Sheffield: T. Montgomery, 1809.

Harper, J. Steven. "Wesley's Sermons as Spiritual Formation Documents," *Methodist History* 26 (April 1988) 131-138.

Hunter, Justus. "A Defense of William Burt Pope's Confessional Methodist Theology." *Wesleyan Theological Journal* 54:2 (Fall 2019) 7-17.

Monk, Robert C. *John Wesley: His Puritan Heritage*. Nashville: Abringdon, 1966.

Strand, Greg. "Strands of Thought." https://blogs.efca.org/strands-of-thought/posts/ an-interview-with- fred-sanders

Jackson, Thomas. *Memoirs of the Life and Writings of the Rev. Richard Watson*. 1834. Reprint, New York: Mason and Lane, 1836.

Knudson, Albert. "Henry Clay Sheldon — Theologian." *Methodist Quarterly Review* 108 (March 1925) 175-192.

Langford, Thomas. *Practical Divinity*. Nashville: Abingdon, 1983.

Lee, Luther. *Elements of Theology, or An Exposition of the Divine Origin, Doctrines, Morals, and Institutions of Christ-ianity*. Syracuse, NY: S. Lee, 1856.

Lindström, Harald. *Wesley and Sanctification*. Grand Rapids: Zondervan, 1980.

Lloyd-Jones, David Martyn. *The Puritans: Their origins and successors: addresses delivered at the Puritan and Westminster conferences 1959-1978*. Carlisle, PA: Banner of Truth, 1987.

Locke, John. *A System of Theology*. London: William Nichols, 1862.

Maddox, Randy. *Responsible Grace*. Nashville: Abingdon, 1994.

Miley, John. *Systematic Theology*. 2 vols. 1893. Reprint, Peabody, MA: Hendrickson, 1989.

Mitton, C. Leslie. *A Clue to Wesley's Sermons*. London: Epworth, 1951.

Moss, Richard Waddy. *The Rev. W. B. Pope, D. D.; Theologian and Saint*. London: Robert Culley, 1903. Reprint, Wilmore, KY: First Fruits, 2021.

Oden Thomas C. *John Wesley's Teachings*. 4 vols. Grand Rapids: Zondervan, 2012-2014.

_____. *Doctrinal Standards in the Wesleyan Tradition*. Grand Rapids: Francis Asbury, 1988.

_____. *The Transforming Power of Grace*. Nashville: Abingdon, 1993.

_____. *Life in the Spirit: Systematic Theology: Volume Three*. San Francisco: HarperCollins, 1992.

Outler, Albert C. *John Wesley*. New York: Oxford, 1964.

Peters, John L. *Christian Perfection and American Methodism*. Nashville: Abingdon, 1956. Reprint, Grand Rapids: Zondervan, 1985, Salem, OH: Schmul, 1995.

Picirilli, Robert. *The Randall House Bible Commentary*. 12 vols. Nashville: Randall House, 1987-2010.

Platt, Frederic. "Perfection (Christian)." *Encyclopedia of Religion and Ethics*. James Hastings, ed. 12 vols. Edinburgh: T & T Clark, 1908-1927.

Pope, William Burt. *A Compendium of Christian Theology*. 3 vols. London: Wesleyan Conference Office, 1880.

_____. *Peculiarities of Methodist Doctrine*. London: Wesleyan Conference Office, 1873.

_____. *A Higher Catechism of Theology*. London: T. Woolmer, 1885.

_____. "A Letter to the Younger Ministers of the Methodist Connexion." Chapter 19 in *Sermons, Addresses, and Charges*. London: Wesleyan Conference Office, 1878. This was also published as a separate tract.

Ralston, Thomas N. *Elements of Divinity*. 1924. Reprint, Salem, OH: Schmul, 1971.

Raymond, Miner. *Systematic Theology*. 3 vols. Cincinnati: Cranston & Stowe, 1877-1879.

Reasoner, Vic. "Assurance or Presumption? Early Attempts to Reconstruct Methodist Doctrine: 1803-1809."*Wesleyan Theological Journal* 44:2 (Fall 2009) 103-119.

_____. "How *Wesleyan* is the Wesley Bible?" *The Arminian Magazine* 12:2 (Fall 1994) 1-4.

_____. "The Earle and Clarke Exposition." *The Arminian Magazine* 12:1 (Spring 1994) 5-8.

_____. "Reviews." *The Arminian Magazine* 19:2 (Fall 2001) 11-12.

_____. "Reviews." *The Arminian Magazine* 27:2 (Fall 2009) 16-17.

Rudolf, L. C. *Francis Asbury*. Nashville: Abingdon, 1966.

Rupp, Richard, and Mark Minnick. "Has He a Horse? The Saga of the Circuit Riders." *Faith for the Family* (July/Aug 1976) 16-19.

Ruth, Lester. *A Little Heaven Below: Worship at Early Methodist Quarterly Meetings*. Nashville: Kingswood, 2000.

Sanders, Fred. "The Mind of William Burt Pope (1822-1903)." http://scriptoriumdaily.com/the-mind-of-william-burt-pope-1822-1903/

Sangster, W. E. "The Church's One Privation." *Religion in Life* 18:4 (1949) 493-507.

_____. *The Path to Perfection.* London: Hodder and Stoughton, 1943.

_____. *The Pure in Heart.* 1954. Reprint, Salem, OH: Schmul, 1984.

Schaeffer, Edith. *The Tapestry.* Waco, TX: Word, 1981.

Scott, Leland Howard. "Methodist Theology in America in the Nineteenth Century." PhD diss, Yale University, 1954.

Smith, Timothy L. *Revivalism and Social Reform.* Baltimore: Johns Hopkins, 1980.

Spann, Glen. *Conservatives in the Great Deep of the Methodist Church, 1900-1980.* Wilmore, KY: Francis Asbury Press, 2023.

Stackpole, Everett S. *The Evidence of Salvation.* 1894. Reprint, Evansville, IN: Fundamental Wesleyan, 1994.

Stanglin, Keith D. and Thomas H. McCall. *Jacob Arminius: Theologian of Grace.* New York: Oxford University Press, 2012.

Staples, Rob L. "A Rose is a Rose is (Not Always) a Rose." *Holiness Today* 1:10 (October 1999) 25.

Steele, Daniel. "Why I Am Not a Premillennialist." *The Methodist Review* 93 (May-June 1911) 405-415.

_____. *A Substitute for Holiness or Antinomianism Revived; or the Theology of the So-Called Plymouth Brethren Examined and Refuted.* 3rd ed. 1899. Reprint, Salem, OH: Schmul, 1980. Mistakenly reprinted as *Steele's Answers.*

_____. *A Defense of Christian Perfection or a Criticism of Dr. James Mudge's "Growth in Holiness Toward Perfection."* 1896. Reprint, Salem, OH: Schmul, 1984.

Stevens, Abel. *Illustrated History of Methodism*. 2 vols. London: James Haggar, 1873.

_____. *Life and Times of Nathan Bangs, D. D.* New York: Carlton & Porter, 1863.

Strong, Augustus H. *Systematic Theology*. Valley Forge, PA: Judson, 1907.

Summers, Thomas O. *Systematic Theology*. 2 vols. John Tigert, ed. Nashville: Methodist Episcopal Church, South, 1888.

Sutcliffe, Joseph. *A Commentary on the Old and New Testament*. 2 vols. 1834. Reprint, Salem, OH: Allegheny, 2000.

_____. *The Paternal Catechism of the Christian Religion*. London: Hamilton, Adams, and Co, 1847.

_____. *The Doctrines of Justification by Faith, of Regeneration, of Assurance and of Present Salvation, Illustrated and Enforced in Four Sermons*. Halifax: Holden and Dowson, 1806.

Telford, John. *Wesley's Veterans*. 7 vols. London: Robert Culley, 1912-1914. Reprint, Salem, OH: Schmul, 1976.

_____. *The Life of John Wesley*. New York: Eaton and Mains, 1886.

Terry, Milton S. *Biblical Hermeneutics*. 2nd ed. 1885. Reprint, Grand Rapids: Zondervan, 1974.

Tracy, Wesley. *When Adam Clarke Preached, People Listened*. Kansas City: Beacon Hill, 1981.

Treffry, Richard. *A Treatise on Christian Perfection*. 1797. Reprint, Salem, OH: Schmul, 1992.

Treffry, Richard, Jr. *Letters on the Atonement*. 2nd ed. London: Wesleyan Conference Office, 1845. Reprinted by Schmul, 2021.

_____. *Lectures of the Evidences of Christianity*. London: John Mason, 1839

_____. *An Inquiry into the Eternal Sonship of Our Lord Jesus Christ*. London: John Mason, 1837.

Tuttle, Robert G. Jr. *Mysticism in the Wesleyan Tradition*. Grand Rapids: Francis Asbury, 1989.

Van Die, Marguerite. *An Evangelical Mind: Nathanael Burwash and the Methodist Tradition in Canada, 1839-1918*. Kingston: McGill-Queen's University Press, 1989.

Wainwright, Arthur. *Mysterious Apocalypse*. Nashville: Abingdon, 1993.

Wakefield, Samuel. *Christian Theology*. 1862. Reprinted as two volumes. Salem, OH: Schmul, 1985.

Watson, Kevin M. *The Class Meeting*. Wilmore, KY: Seedbed, 2014.

_____ and Scott T. Kisker. *The Band Meeting*. Franklin, TN: Seedbed, 2017.

Watson, Richard. *A Biblical and Theological Dictionary*. New York: Carlton & Porter, 1832. Reprint, Evansville, IN: Fundamental Wesleyan Publishers, 2000.

_____. *Conversations for the Young: Designed to Promote the Profitable Reading of the Holy Scriptures*. John Mason, 1830.

_____. *An Exposition of the Gospels of St. Matthew and St. Mark*. London: Wesleyan Conference Office, 1833.

_____. *The Life of the Rev. John Wesley, A. M.* London: John Mason, 1831.

_____. *Remarks on the Eternal Sonship of Christ; and the Use of Reason in Matters of Revelation: Suggested by Several Passages in Dr. Adam Clarke's*

Commentary on the New Testament. In a Letter to a Friend. London: T. Cordeaux, 1818.

_____. *Sermons and Sketches of Sermons.* 2 vols. New York: Carlton & Porter, 1851.

_____. *Theological Institutes.* 2 vols. 1823-1829. Reprint, New York: Hunt & Eaton, 1889. Reprint, Bellingham, WA: Lexham, 2018 with a new introduction by Ben Witherington III.

_____. *The Works of the Rev. Richard Watson.* Thomas Jackson, ed. 2nd ed. 12 vols. London: John Mason, 1834-1837.

Wesley, John. *The Bicentennial Edition of the Works of John Wesley.* Frank Baker and Richard P. Heitzenrater, eds. 26 vols. to date. Nashville: Abingdon, 1976-.

_____, ed. *A Christian Library: Consisting of Extracts from and Abridgments of the Choicest Pieces of Practical Divinity which have been published in the English Tongue in Thirty Volumes.* 2nd ed. London: Thomas Cordeux, 1819-1826.

_____. *Explanatory Notes Upon the New Testament.* 1754. Reprint, Salem, OH: Schmul, 1976.

_____. *Explanatory Notes Upon the Old Testament.* 3 vols. 1765. Reprint, Salem, OH: Schmul. 1975.

_____. *The Works of John Wesley.* Thomas Jackson, ed. Third edition. 14 vols. 1872. Reprint, Grand Rapids: Zondervan, 1979.

_____. *The Works of the Rev. John Wesley.* Joseph Benson, ed. 17 vols. London: Thomas Cordeaux, 1812.

Whedon, Daniel D. *The Freedom of the Will as a Basis of Human Responsibility and a Divine Government.* 1864. Reprint, Eugene, OR: Wipf & Stock, 2009.

Williams, Henry W. *An Exposition of St. Paul's Epistle to the Romans*. London: Wesleyan Conference Office, 1869.

_____. *A Manual of Natural and Revealed Theology, Designed Especially for Local Preachers, and Sunday-School Teachers*. London: T. Woolmer, 1882.

Williams, William G. *An Exposition of the Epistle of Paul to the Romans*. New York: Eaton & Mains, 1902.

Wood, A. Skevington. *The Burning Heart*. Minneapolis: Bethany, 1967.

An *Ad Fontes* Printing Agenda

- We need a critical edition of Jacob Arminius. He wrote in Dutch and Latin. In some cases the Latin was translated from the Dutch and the English translated from the Latin. The result is a very wooden translation. We need a fresh translation from Dutch to English as Stephen Gunter did for the *Declaration of Sentiments* by Arminius.
- Reprint *John Wesley's Commentary on the Bible*, last done by Zondervan in 1990.
- Translation of the approximate 400 unpublished French and English sermon manuscripts of John Fletcher.
- Reprint W. B. Pope's major works, especially his 3-volume *Compendium* and his *Catechism.*
- Print the dissertations of Dunlap and Scott.
- Reprint James Mudge, *Growth in Holiness Toward Perfection*. New York: Eaton and Mains, 1895. Daniel Steele wrote a rebuttal, *A Defense of Christian Perfection* (1896). Both men were partially right. However, the Steele book has been reprinted. It needs to be read in connection with the Mudge book as essentially a debate between older Methodism and newer holiness theology.

A Suggested Starter List for 21st Century Classic Methodists

- Wesley's *Standard Sermons.*
- Wesley's *Notes upon the New Testament.*
- *The Works of John Fletcher.*
- Clarke, *Commentary.*
- Collins, *A Real Christian: The Life of John Wesley.*
- Watson, *Theological Institutes.*
- Watson, *Theological Dictionary.*
- Pope, *The Prayers of St. Paul.*
- Telford, *Wesley's Veterans.* 7 vols.
- Peters, *Christian Perfection and American Methodism.*
- Chiles, *Theological Transition in American Methodism.*
- Stanglin and McCall, *Jacob Arminius: Theologian of Grace.*
- Oden, *John Wesley's Teachings.* 4 vols.
- Oden, *The Transforming Power of Grace.*

This list is limited to what is in print. Therefore you can mark what you want and leave it for your family to find. Then they will know what to get you for a gift. For their convenience, the phone number for Schmul Publishers is 800-772-6657.

I became convinced that the best way to supply classic Methodist exegesis to busy pastors was in the form of biblical commentaries. Nearly all commentaries are moderately to completely Calvinistic in their orientation. In January 2000 I started research for a series of *Fundamental Wesleyan Commentaries*. I attempted to interact with all extant classic Methodist literature on the text. Here is what I have produced to date:

- Romans (2002). Second edition, two-volumes (2020).
- Revelation (2005). Second edition, two-volumes (2023).
- 1-2 Peter (2017)
- 1 John – Jude (2016)
- Ephesians (2020).
- Philippians & Colossians (2023).
- Hebrews (2025)

These commentaries are available on Amazon in paper and Kindle format. They are also available in Spanish in paper and Kindle. Some are starting to be printing in Portuguese.

www.ingramcontent.com/pod-product-compliance
Lightning Source LLC
Chambersburg PA
CBHW062102270326
41931CB00013B/3183